ROSES
Original Prints
Mother Earth Series

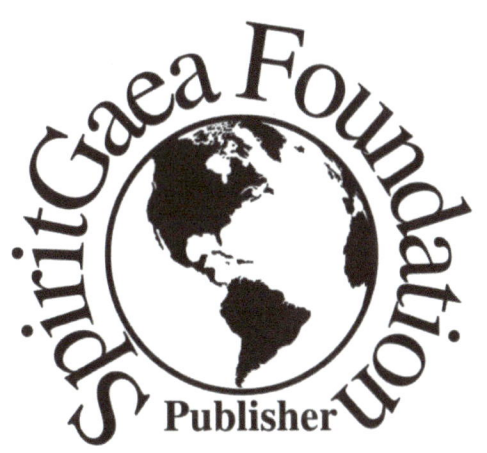
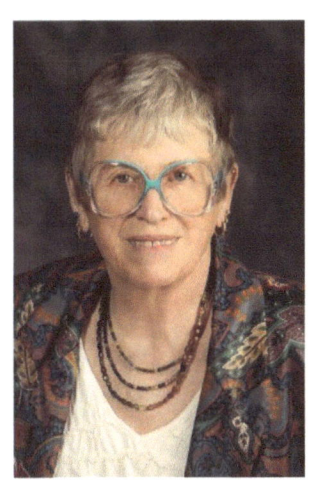

Author Artist   Jeri Lee C.Ht.

Copyright JeriLee.Com
2023
All Rights Reserved
ISBN: 9798388617897

Watercolor Art Originals

Watercolor painting is an expressive and unique form of Art that has been used to create beautiful works throughout history. It involves using thin, transparent water-based paints to create vivid images on paper or canvas surfaces. Watercolor paintings often feature soft color blends and delicate brushstrokes that lend a dreamy, romantic quality to the artwork. The vibrant colors used in this type of painting can evoke strong emotions from viewers, making it a popular choice for many artists seeking to express their innermost feelings through visual means.

Watercolor Art is a beautiful medium to capture the magic and life of nature. Using watercolors, artists can create soft, delicate washes that mimic the subtle colors of plants and animals. Watercolors blend easily with other media, such as ink or pencils, to add texture and detail. With practice, an artist can use watercolor paints to portray flowers, trees, mountains, rivers, and more with realistic depth and color.

This form of Art can bring a unique and beautiful element to any wall in your home. Whether you are looking for a tranquil landscape, vibrant flowers, or abstract shapes, there is sure to be something that captures the spirit of nature and brings joy to your space. This versatile medium will provide an eye-catching addition to any room in your home.

At age 84, I am attempting to replicate Grandma Moses with my unique version of watercolor originals. Please follow my Mother Nature Series. And if they please you, please post me a positive review.
Thank you JeriLee.Com

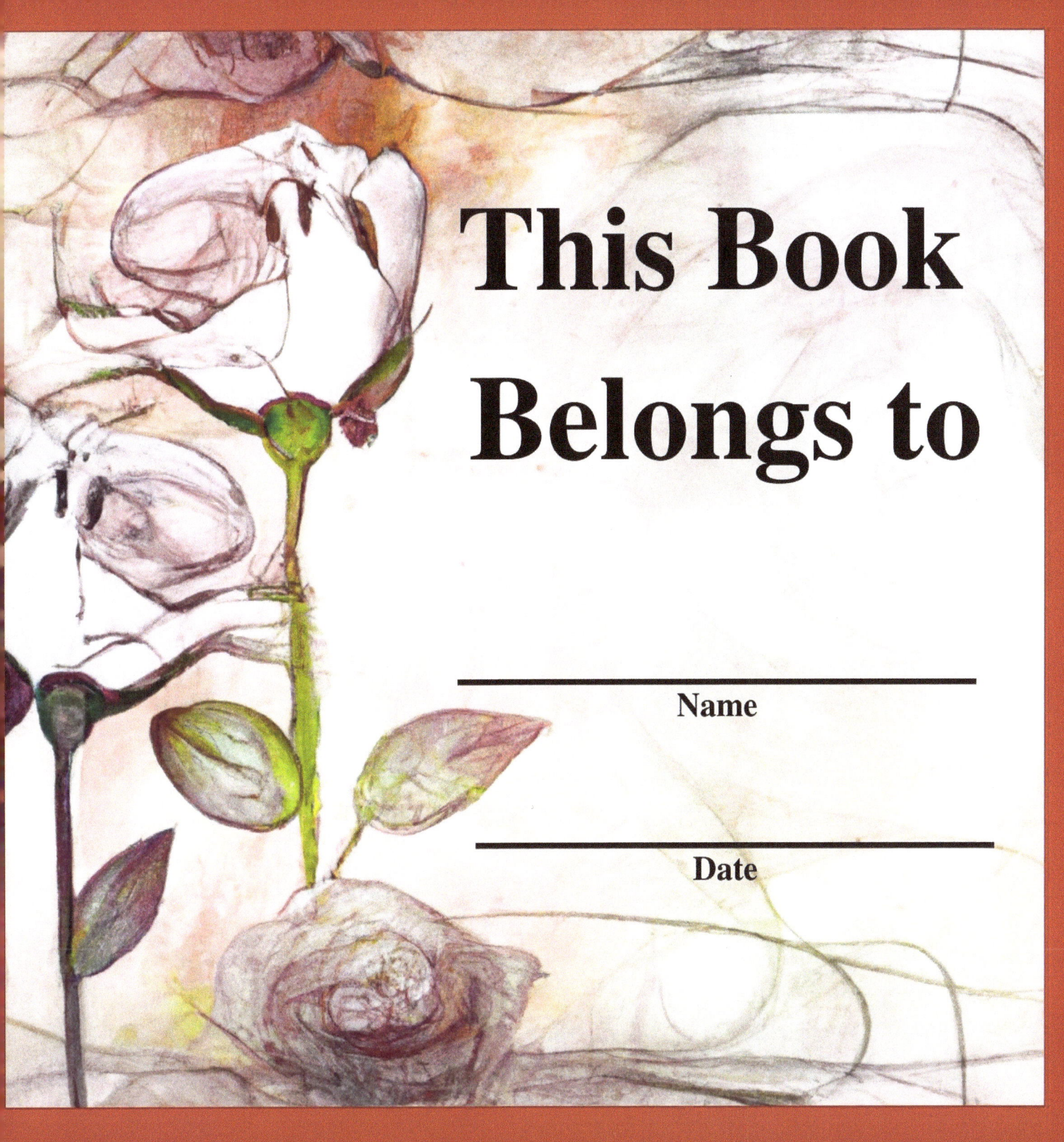

ROSES

Roses are one of the most popular and widely cultivated flowers worldwide. They have been around for centuries, with wide varieties in various colors, shapes, sizes, and fragrances. Roses are often associated with love and romance due to their beauty and fragrance. Roses belong to the family Rosaceae, which includes other flowering plants such as apples, raspberries, cherries, and almonds. Most roses grown today are hybridized from two or more species of wild roses. There are over 100 species of wild roses found throughout North America, Europe, and Asia. Throughout history, the rose has long been regarded as a symbol of love and beauty. Ancient Greeks used it as an aphrodisiac, while Romans believed it was a sign of fertility; both cultures also associated it with Venus—the goddess of love—and Aphrodite—the goddess of beauty. In Christianity, red roses represent martyrdom, while white ones stand for purity or innocence; pink is said to symbolize gracefulness or admiration, while yellow stands for joy or friendship. When selecting roses for your garden, there are several factors you should consider: climate (will vary by region), color preference (reds tend to be hardier than pastels), flower shape (single petals vs. double) size (miniature vs. large blooms) fragrance strength (light scent vs. strong perfume). The type you choose will depend on what kind looks best in your landscape design plan and how much maintenance they require once planted - some types need pruning regularly. In contrast, others can be left alone after planting without any additional care required during the season. In addition to being beautiful ornamental plants that can add interest to gardens, landscaped areas, patios & decks, etc., rose bushes provide food sources for bees & butterflies! Rose hips – which form at the base after each bloom fades away – contain essential vitamins & minerals that birds & mammals rely on during colder months when natural resources may not be available elsewhere. So if you're looking into adding something special but beneficial too, consider growing some beautiful rose bushes!

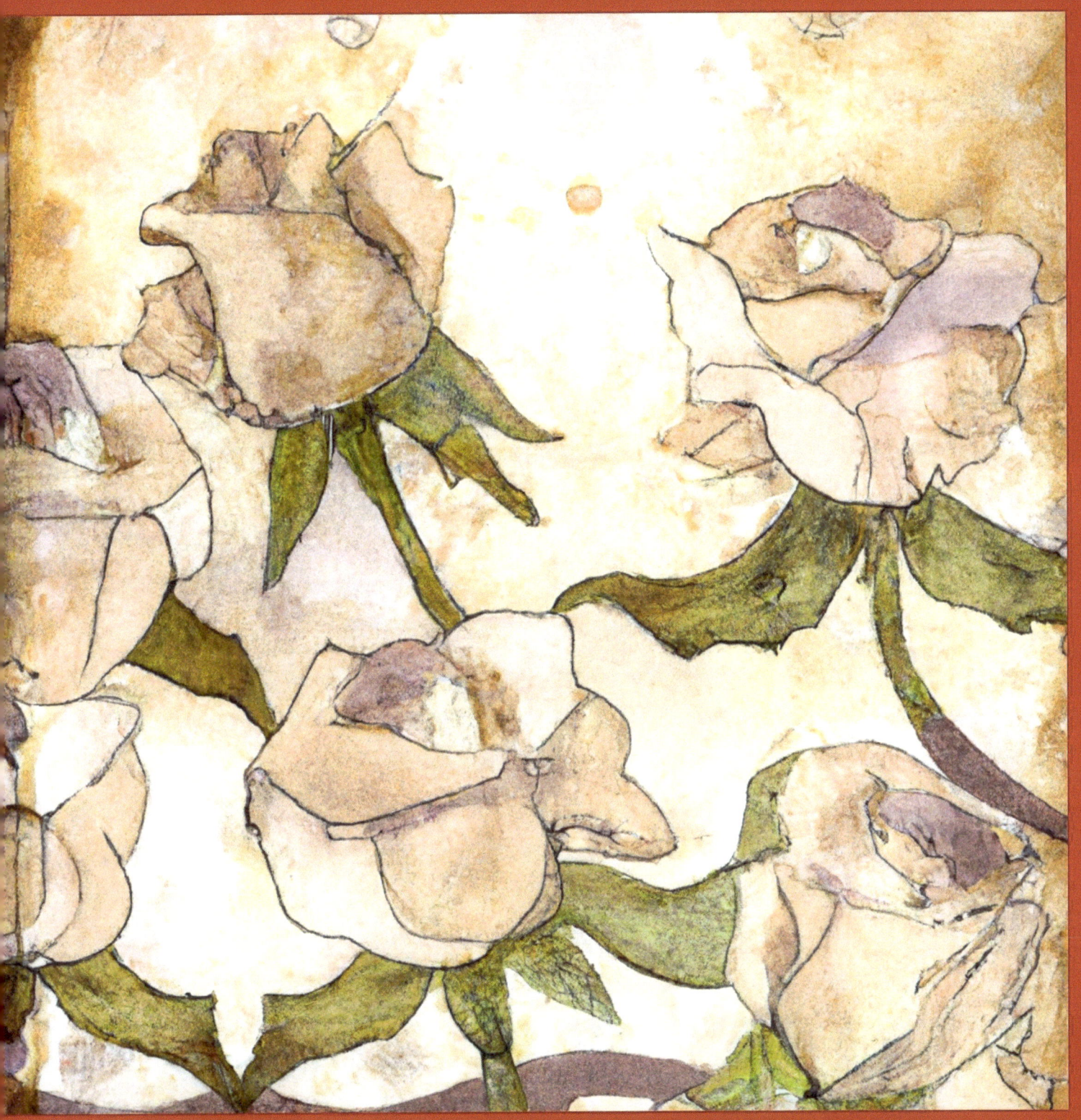

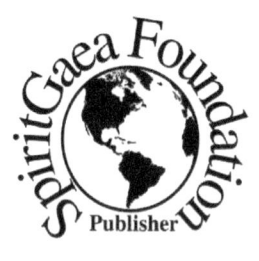

Author Artist

**Original Art
by Jeri Lee**

Copyright Jerilee.com
2022
All rights Reserved

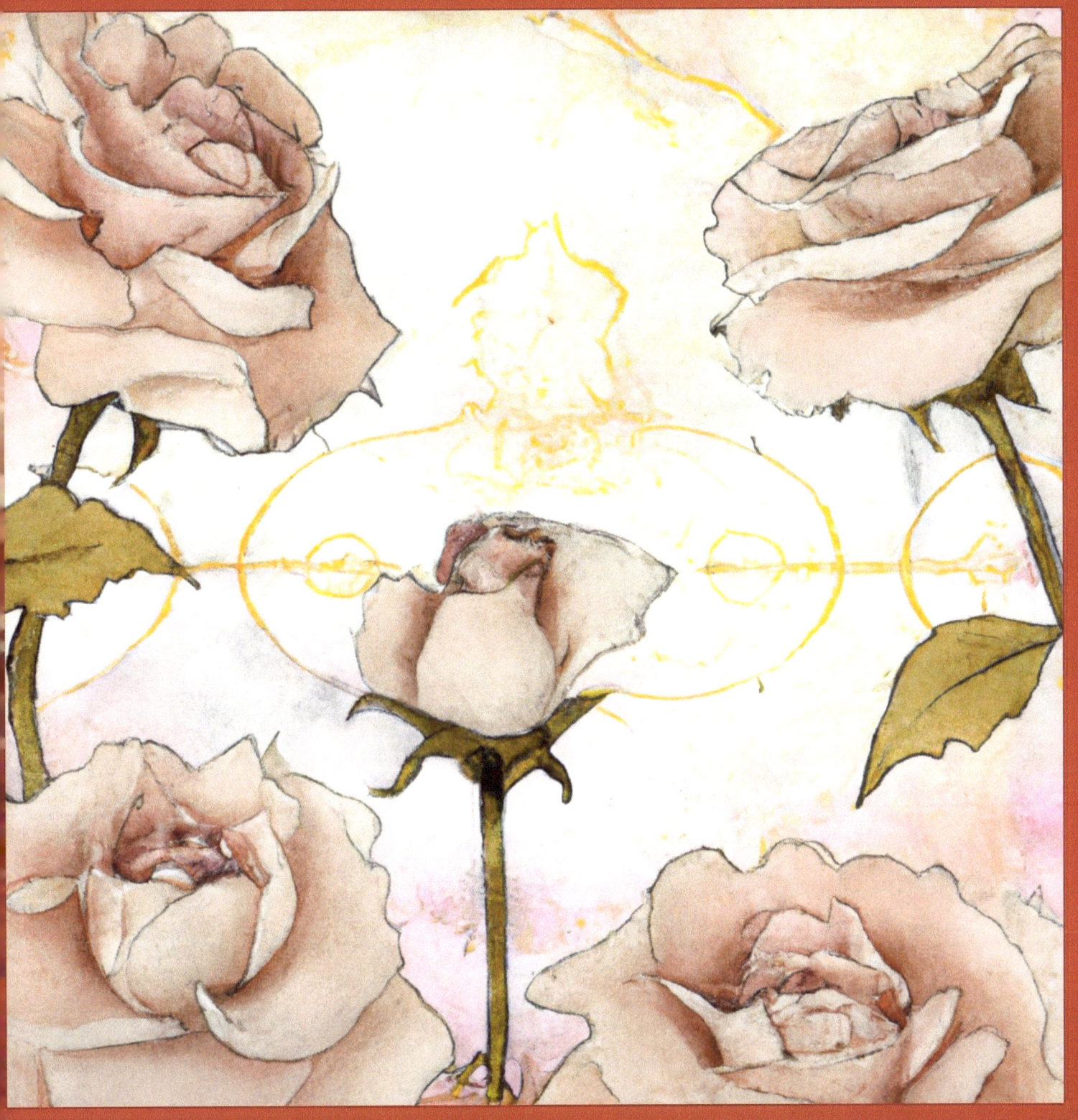

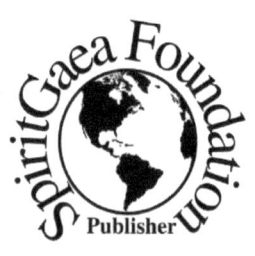

Author Artist

**Original Art
by Jeri Lee**

Copyright Jerilee.com
2022
All rights Reserved

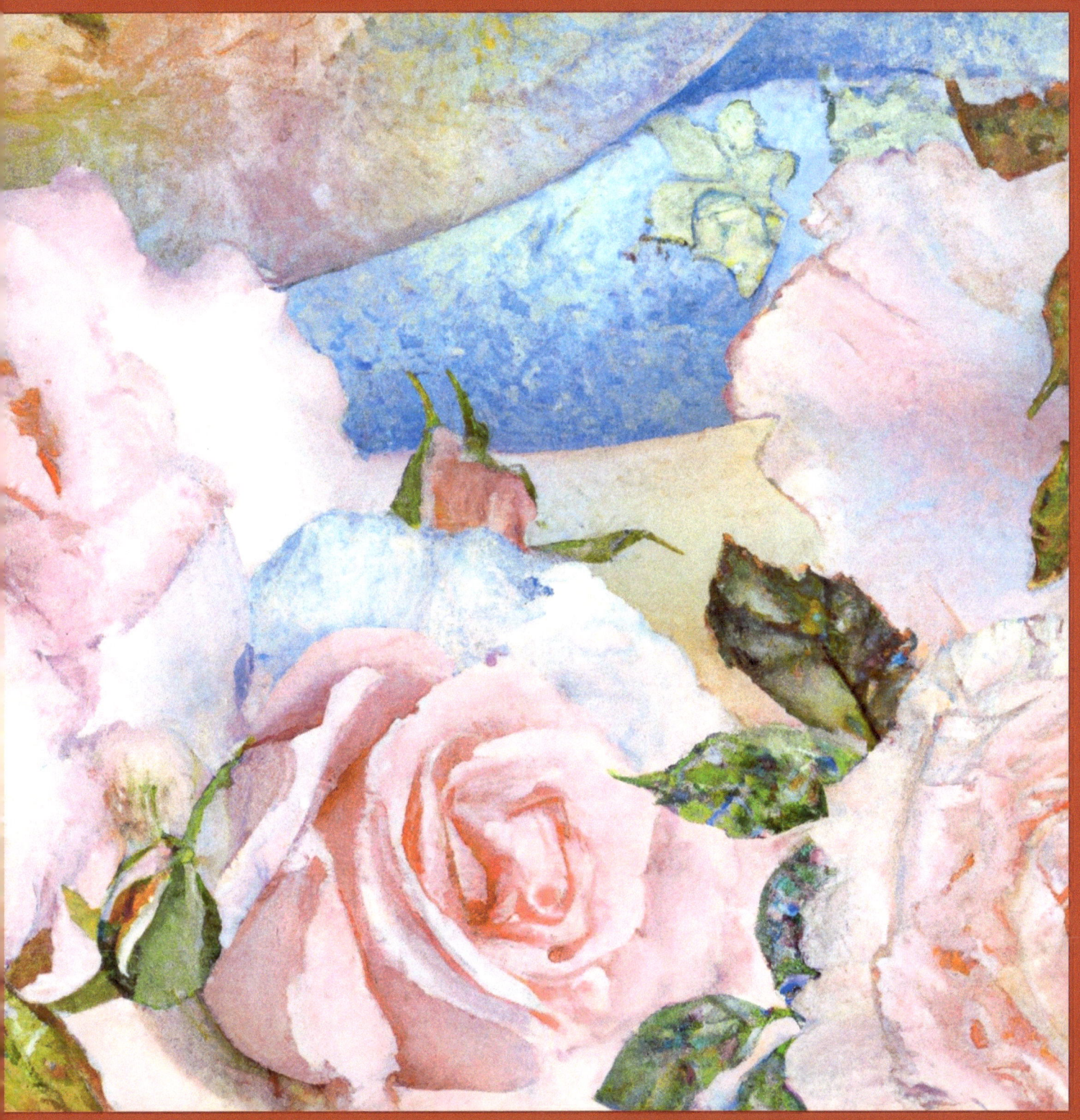

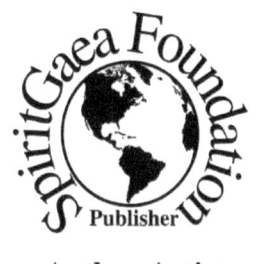
Author Artist

**Original Art
by Jeri Lee**

Copyright Jerilee.com
2022
All rights Reserved

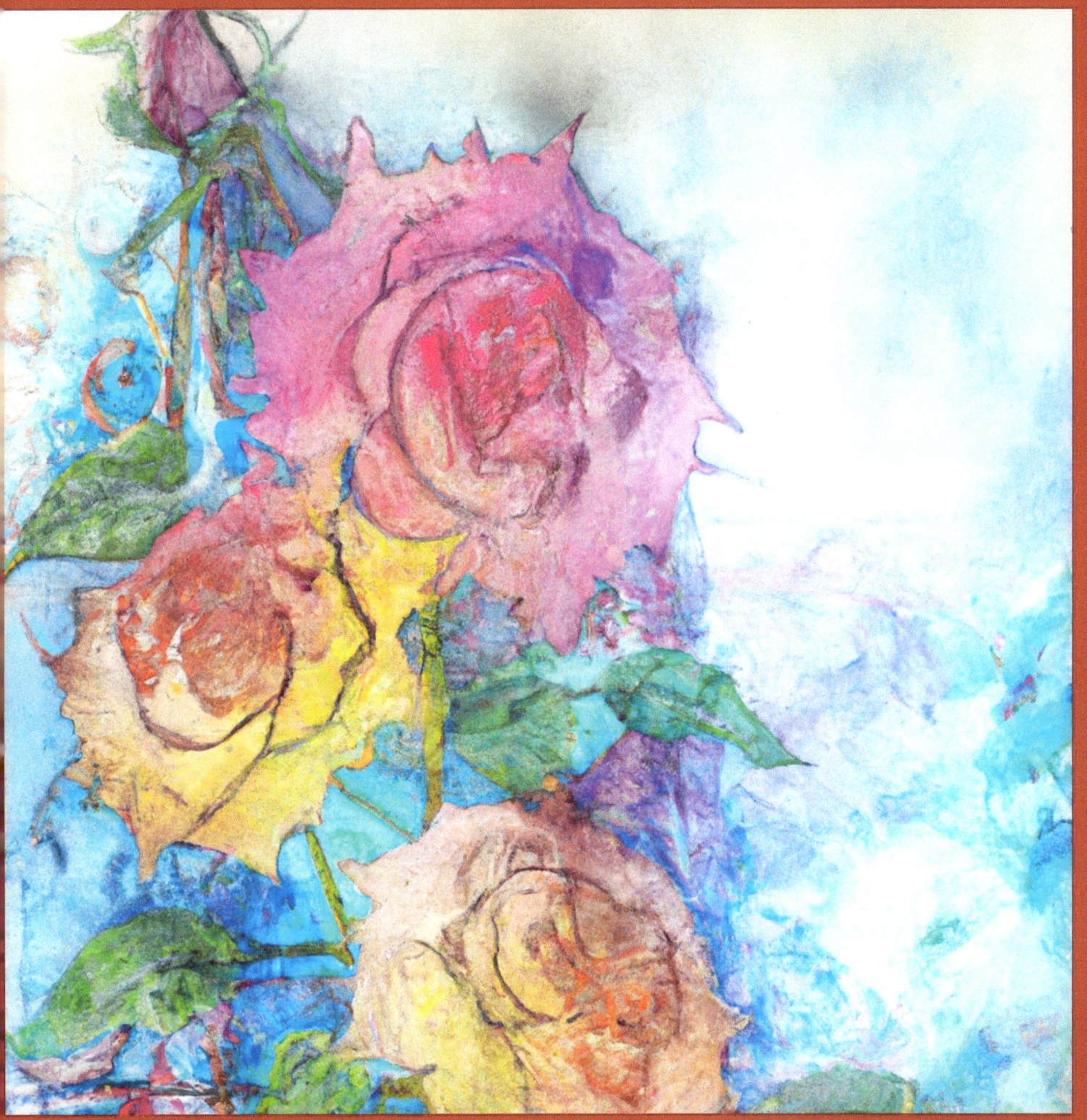

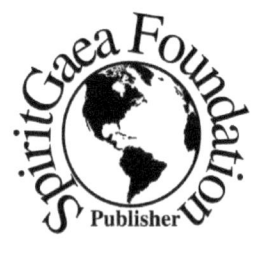

Author Artist

**Original Art
by Jeri Lee**

Copyright Jerilee.com
2022
All rights Reserved

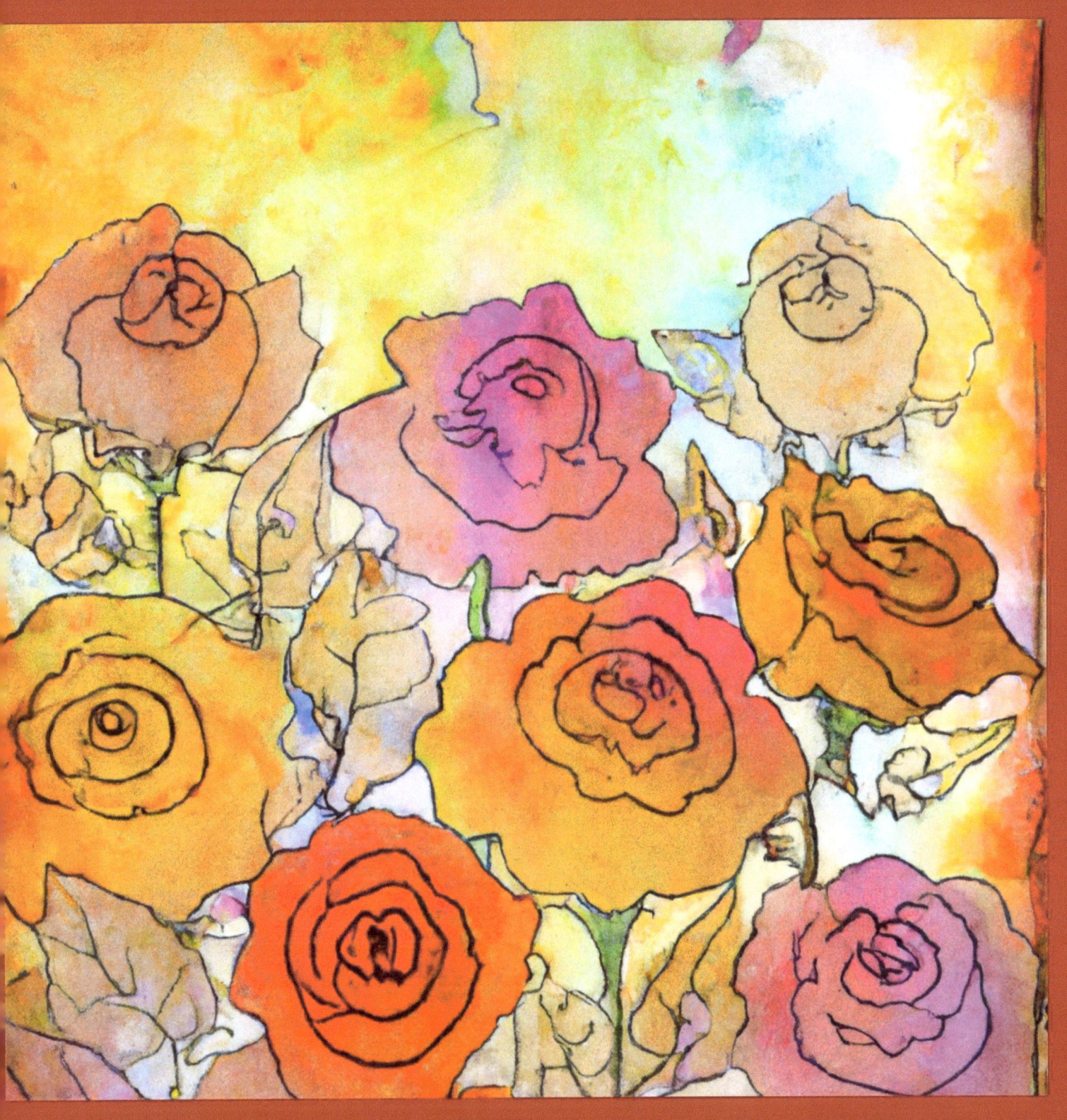

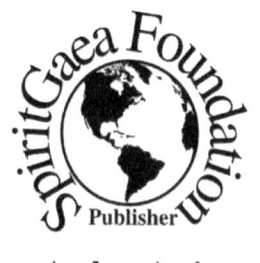

Author Artist

**Original Art
by Jeri Lee**

Copyright Jerilee.com
2022
All rights Reserved

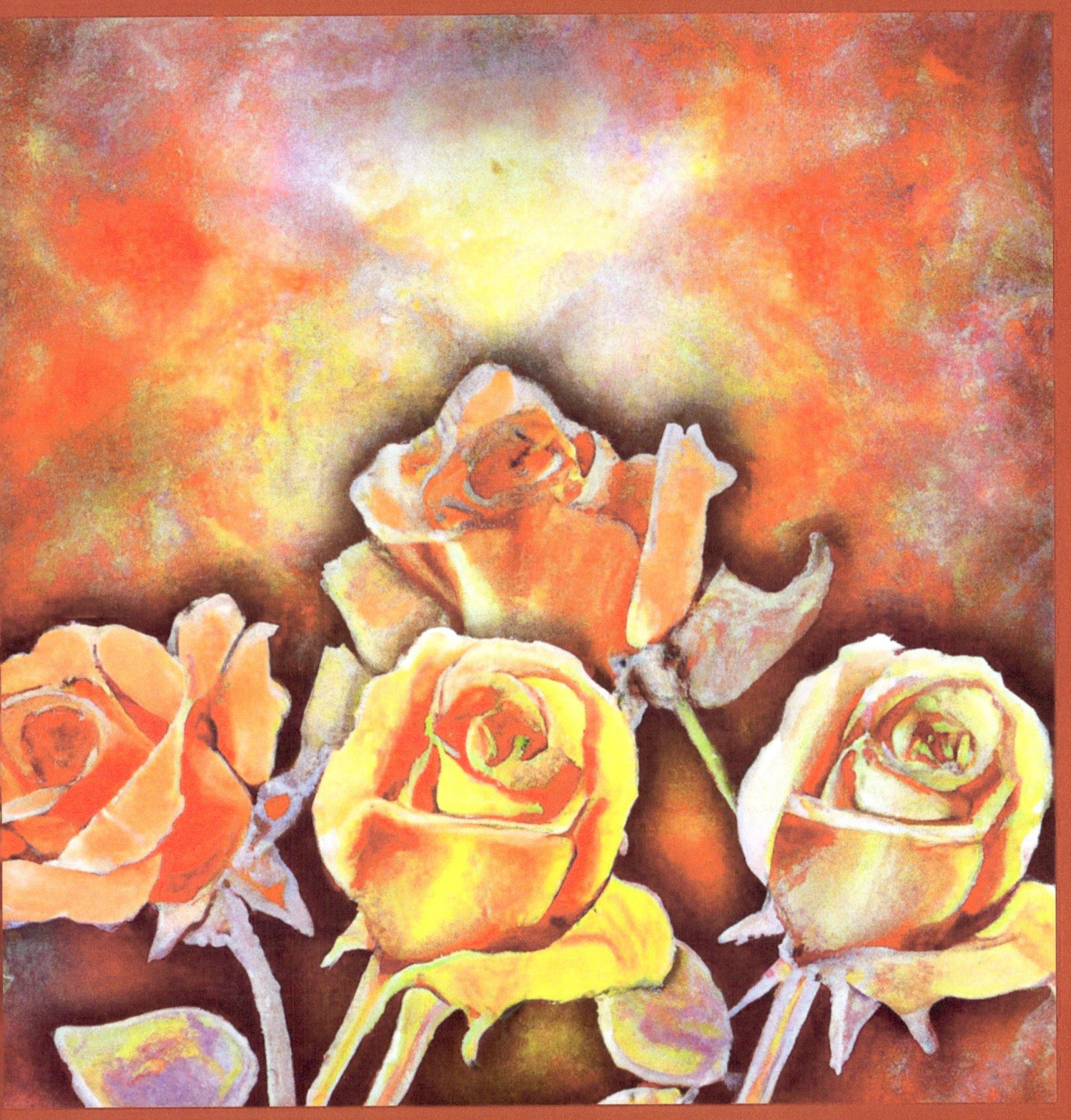

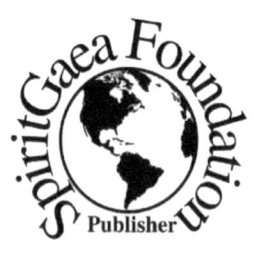

**Original Art
by Jeri Lee**

Copyright Jerilee.com
2022
All rights Reserved

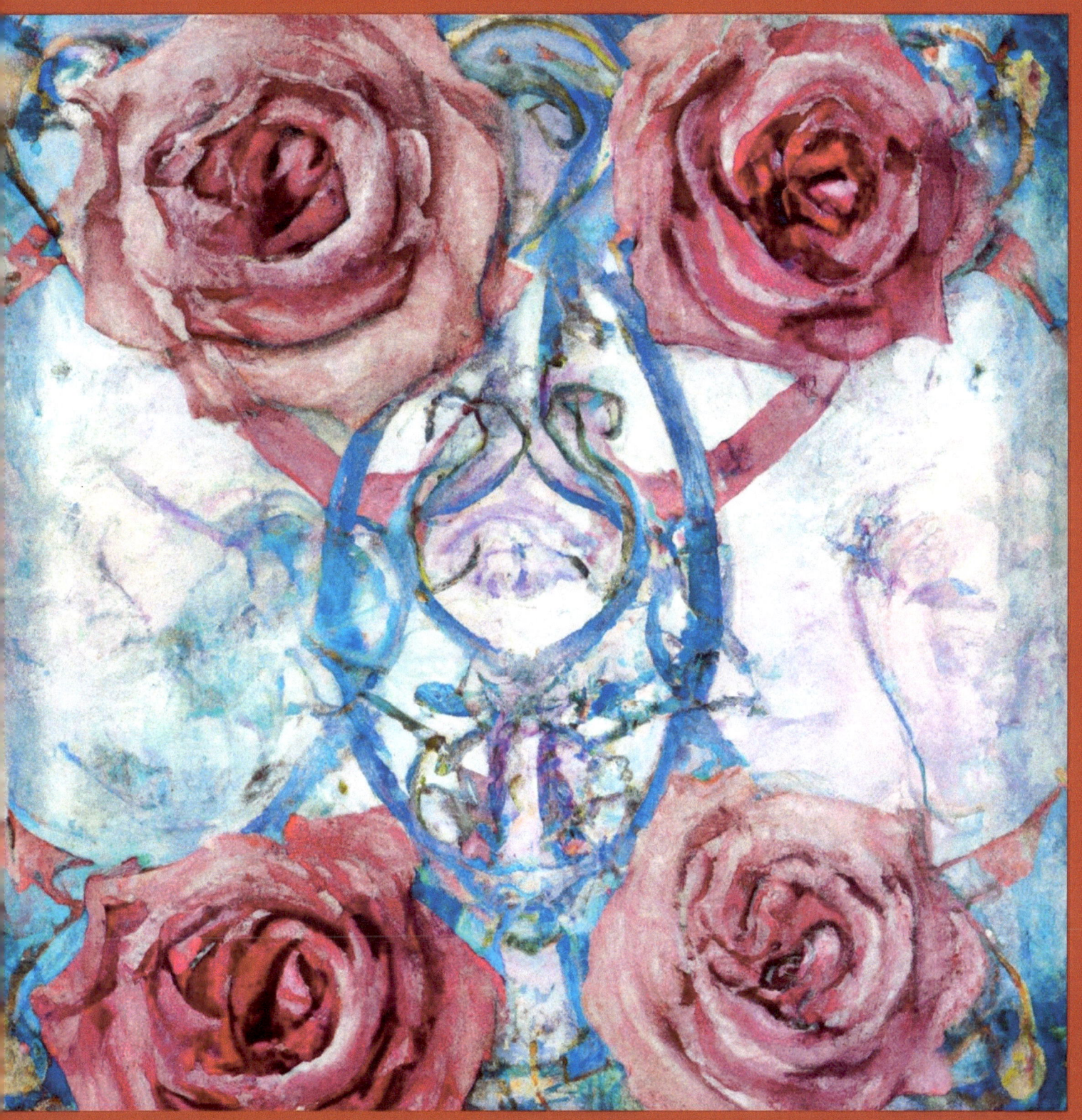

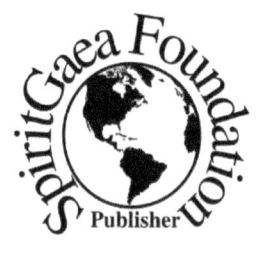

Author Artist

**Original Art
by Jeri Lee**

Copyright Jerilee.com
2022
All rights Reserved

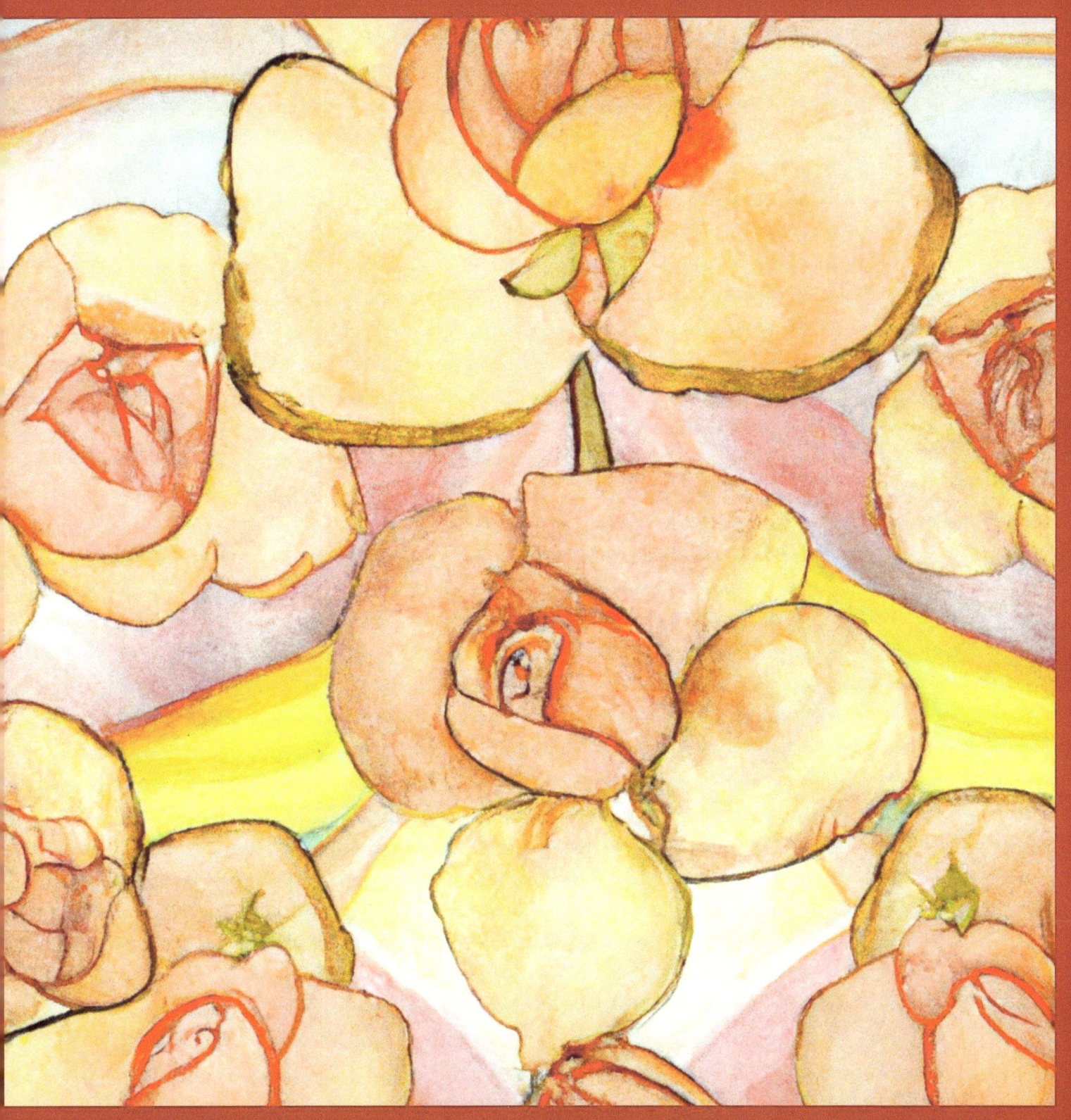

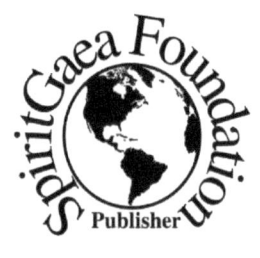

Author Artist

**Original Art
by Jeri Lee**

Copyright Jerilee.com
2022
All rights Reserved

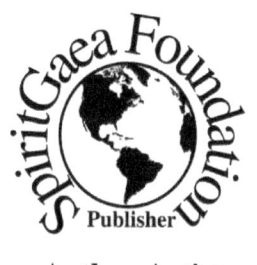
Author Artist

**Original Art
by Jeri Lee**

Copyright Jerilee.com
2022
All rights Reserved

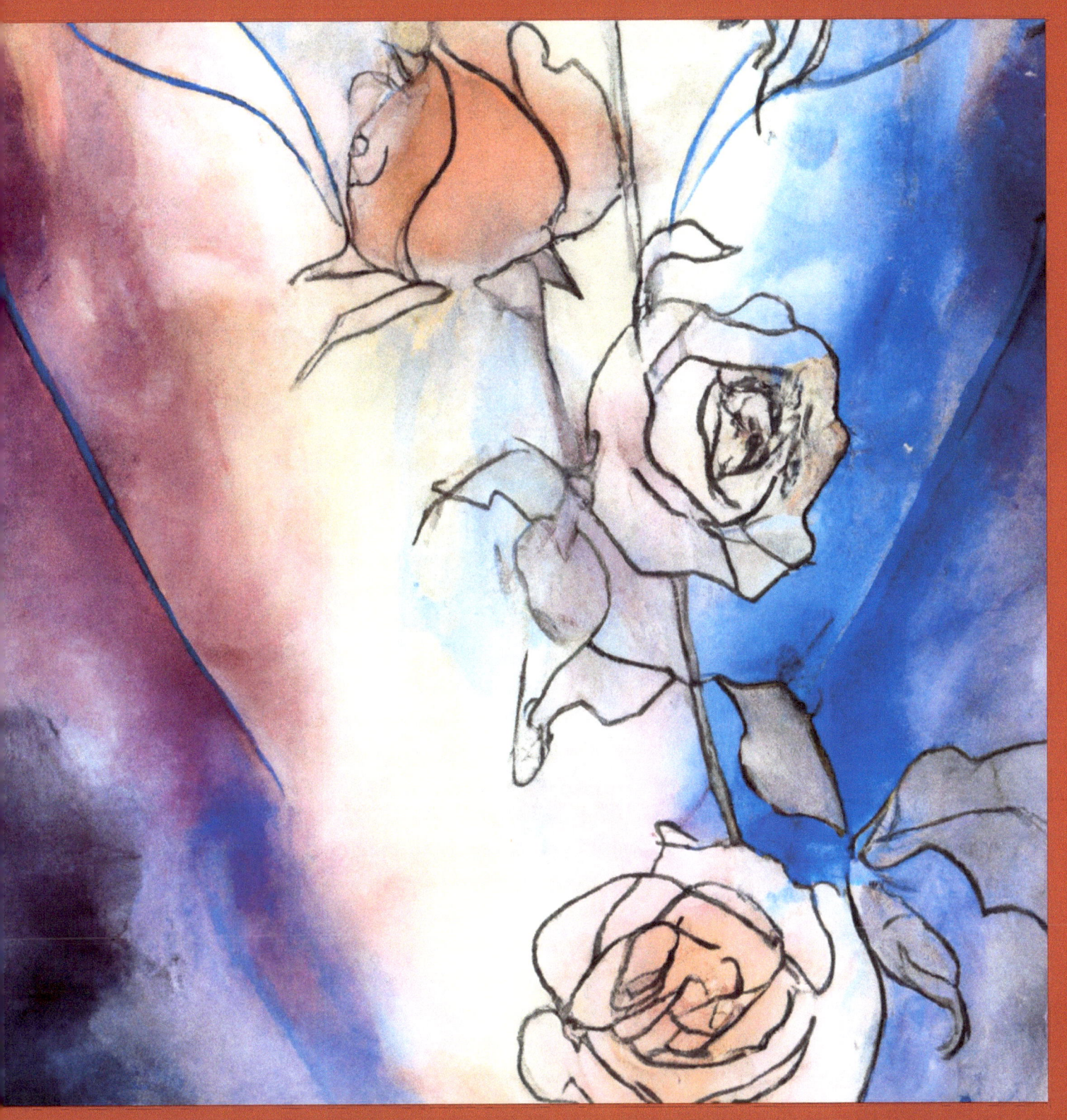

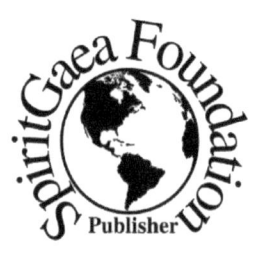

Author Artist

**Original Art
by Jeri Lee**

Copyright Jerilee.com
2022
All rights Reserved

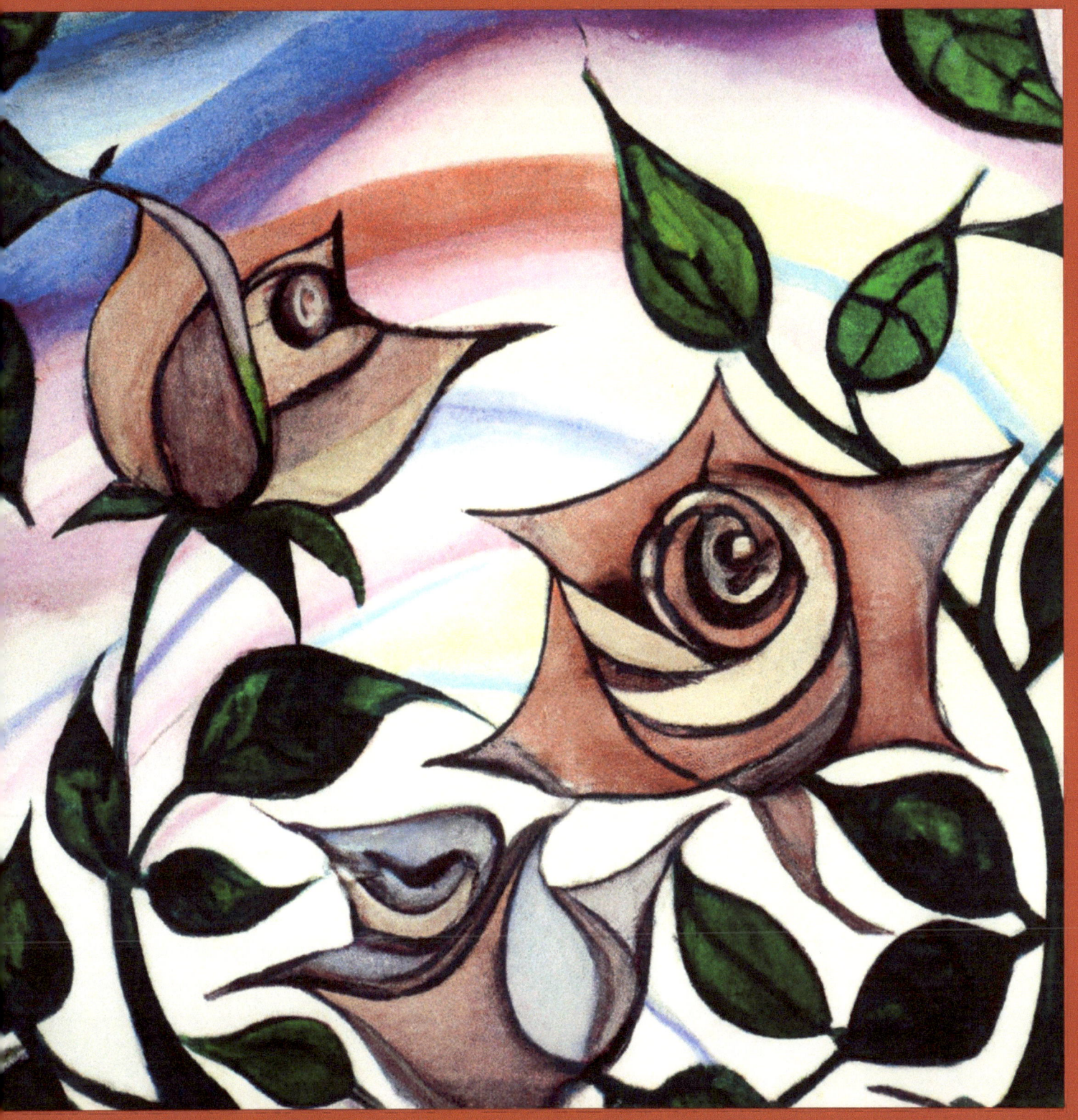

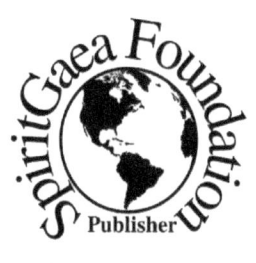

Author Artist

**Original Art
by Jeri Lee**

Copyright Jerilee.com
2022
All rights Reserved

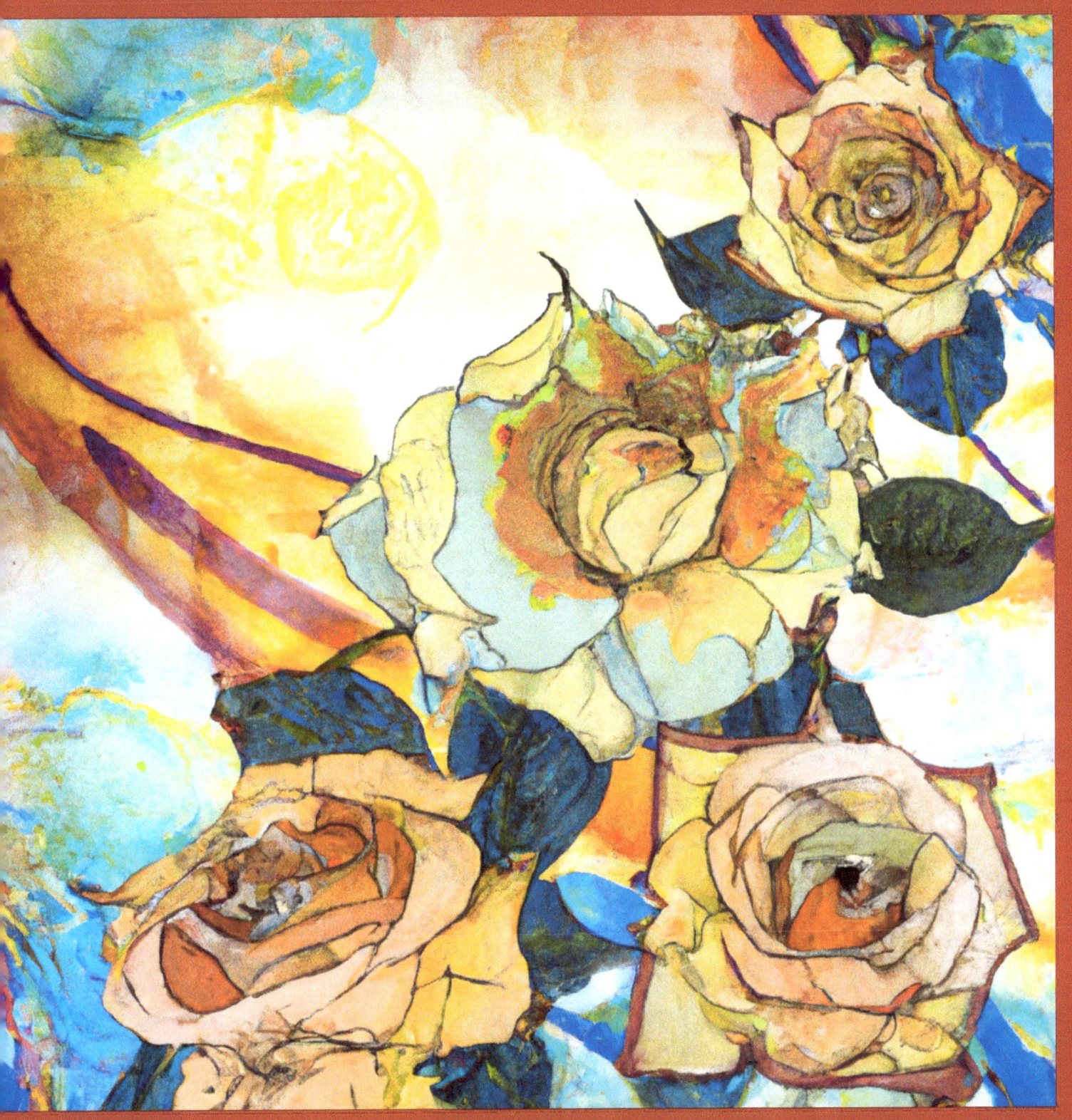

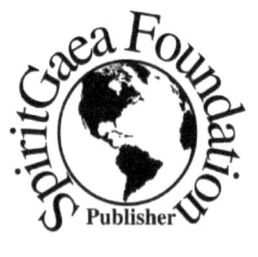

Author Artist

**Original Art
by Jeri Lee**

Copyright Jerilee.com
2022
All rights Reserved

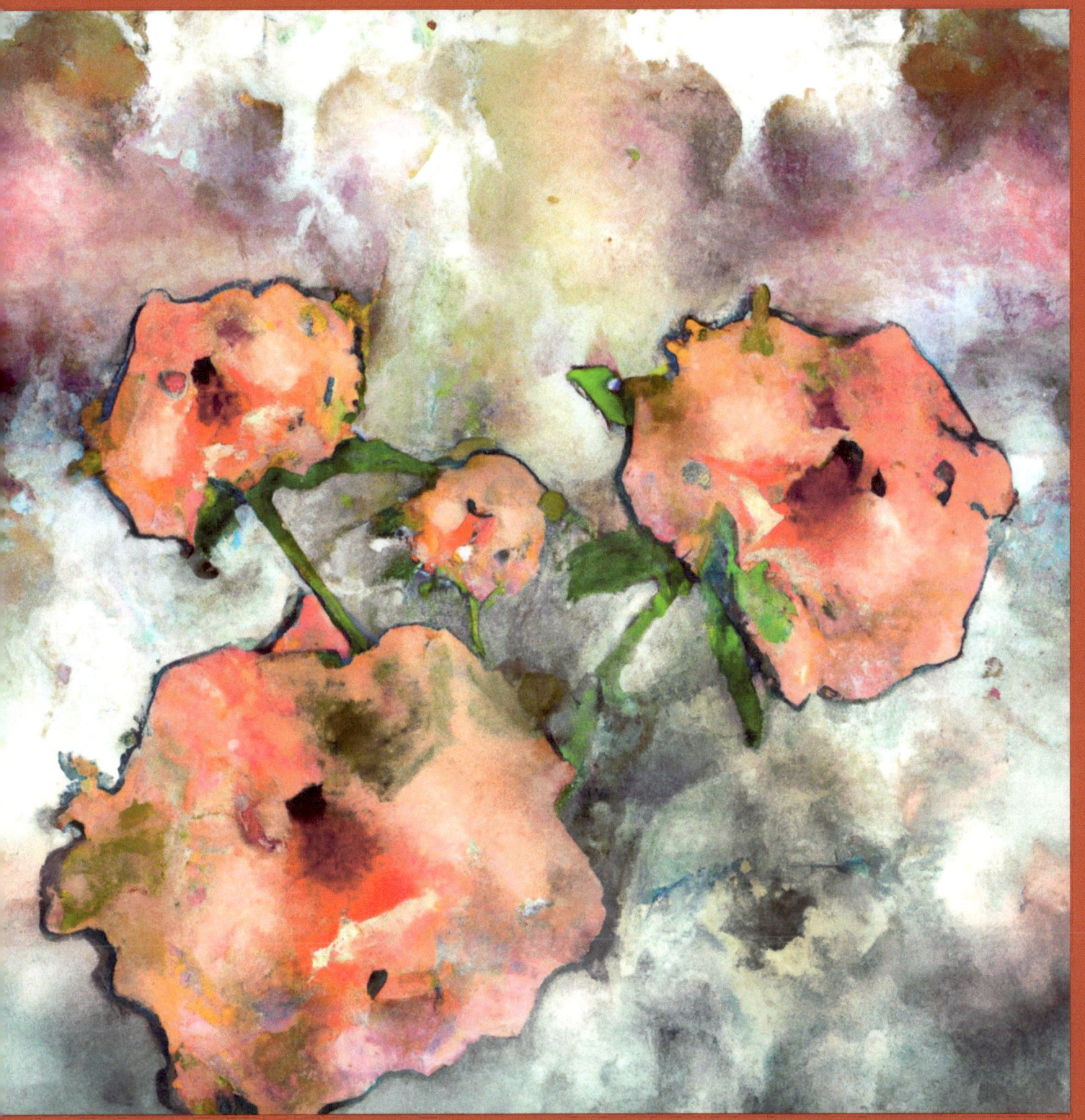

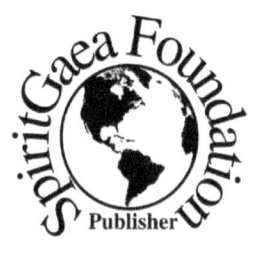

**Original Art
by Jeri Lee**

Copyright Jerilee.com
2022
All rights Reserved

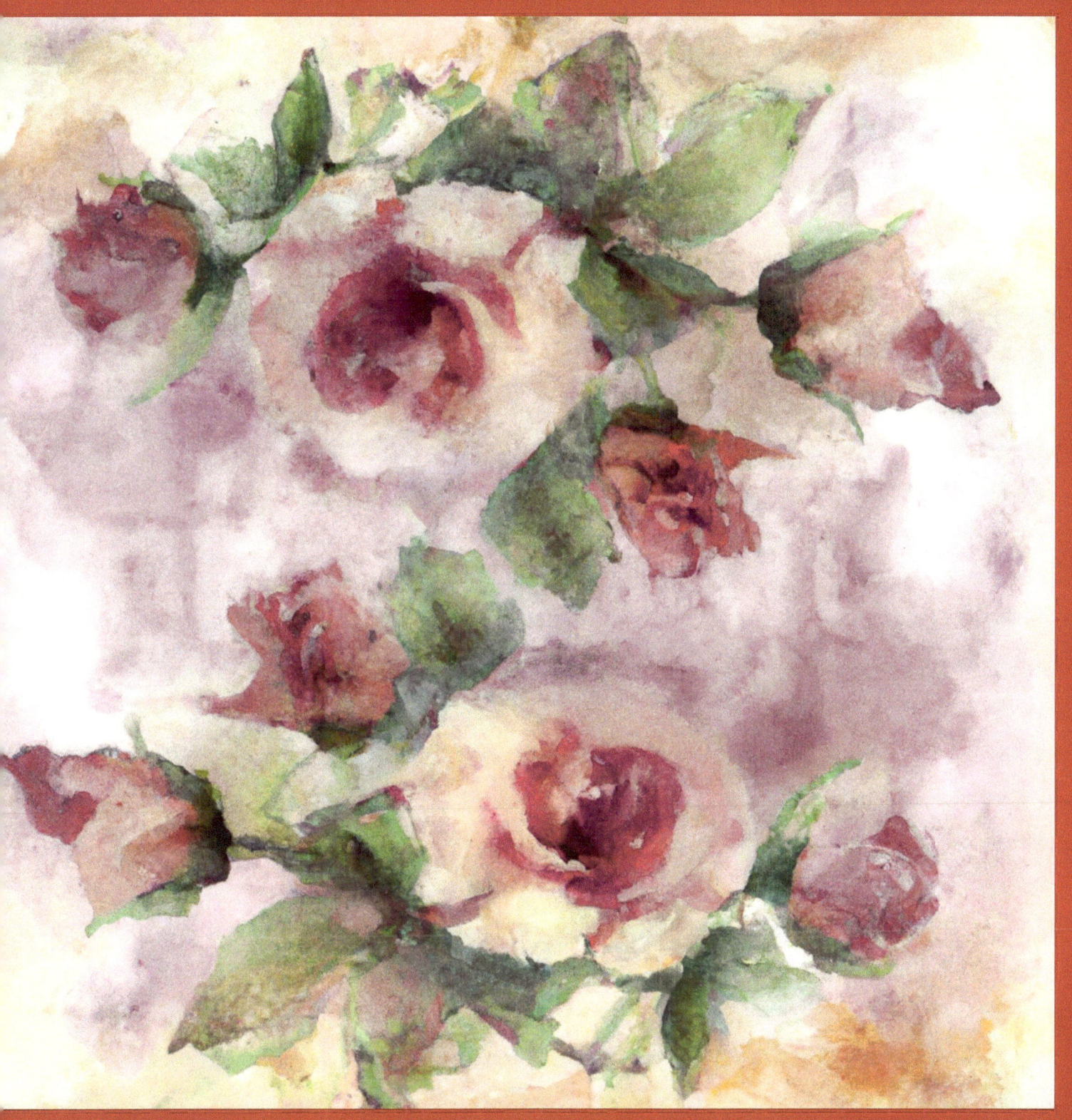

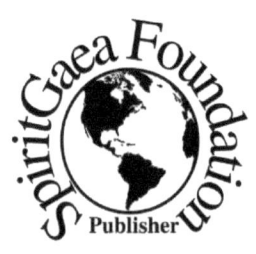

Author Artist

**Original Art
by Jeri Lee**

Copyright Jerilee.com
2022
All rights Reserved

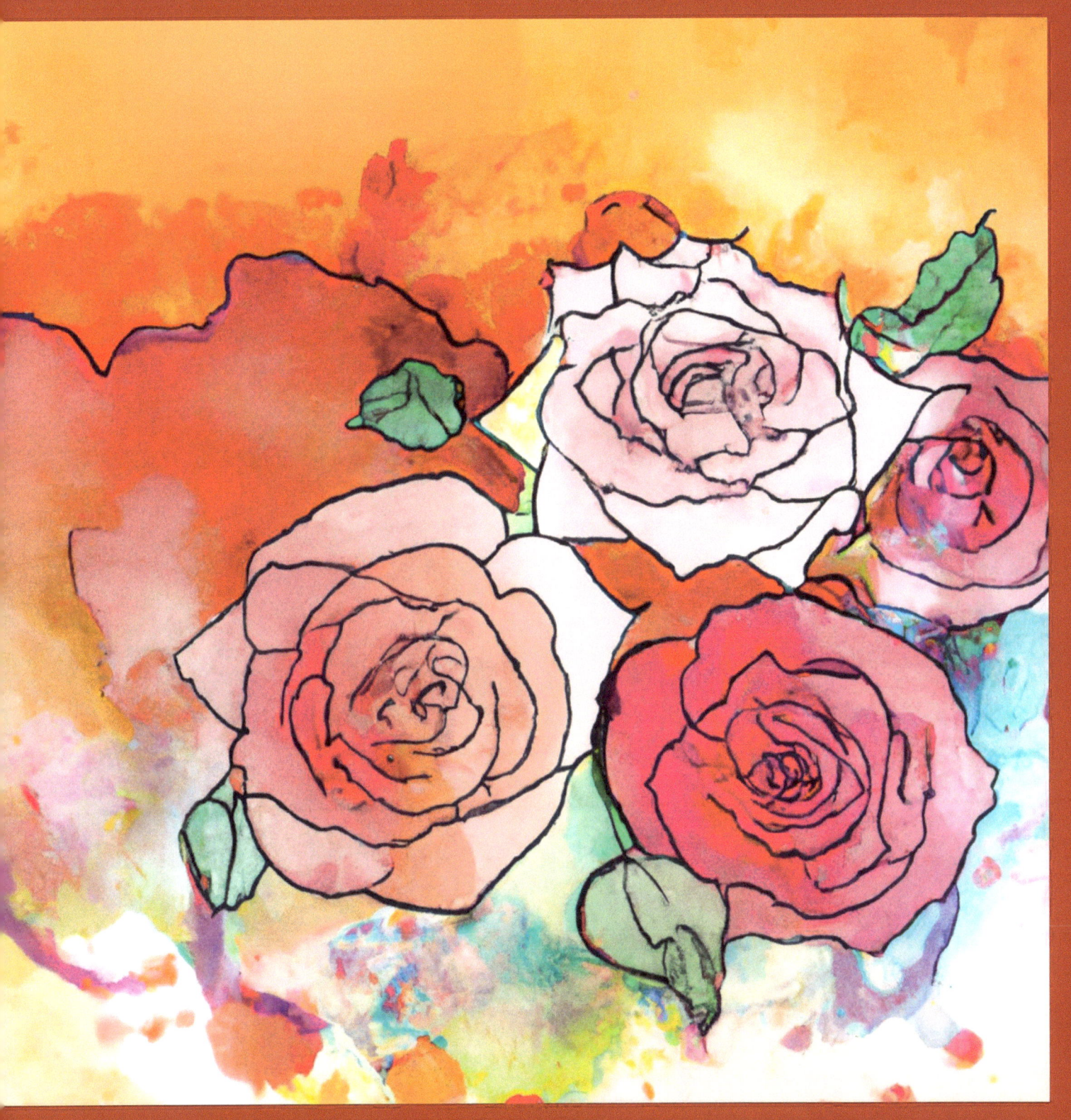

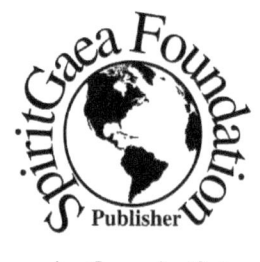

**Original Art
by Jeri Lee**

Copyright Jerilee.com
2022
All rights Reserved

Author Artist

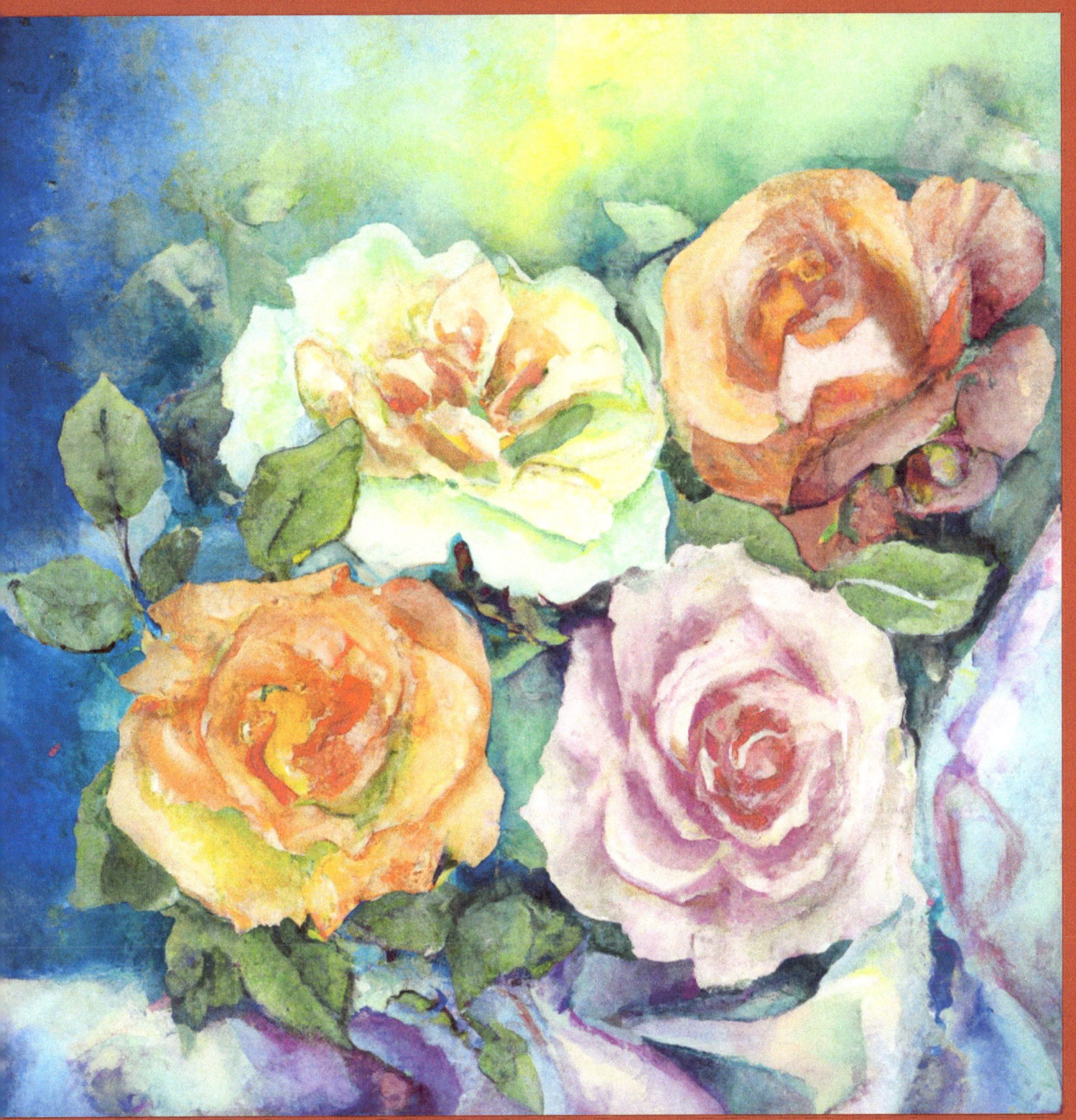

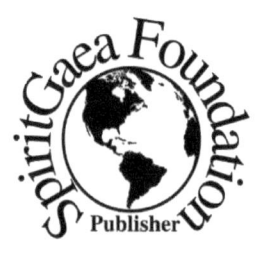
Author Artist

**Original Art
by Jeri Lee**

Copyright Jerilee.com
2022
All rights Reserved

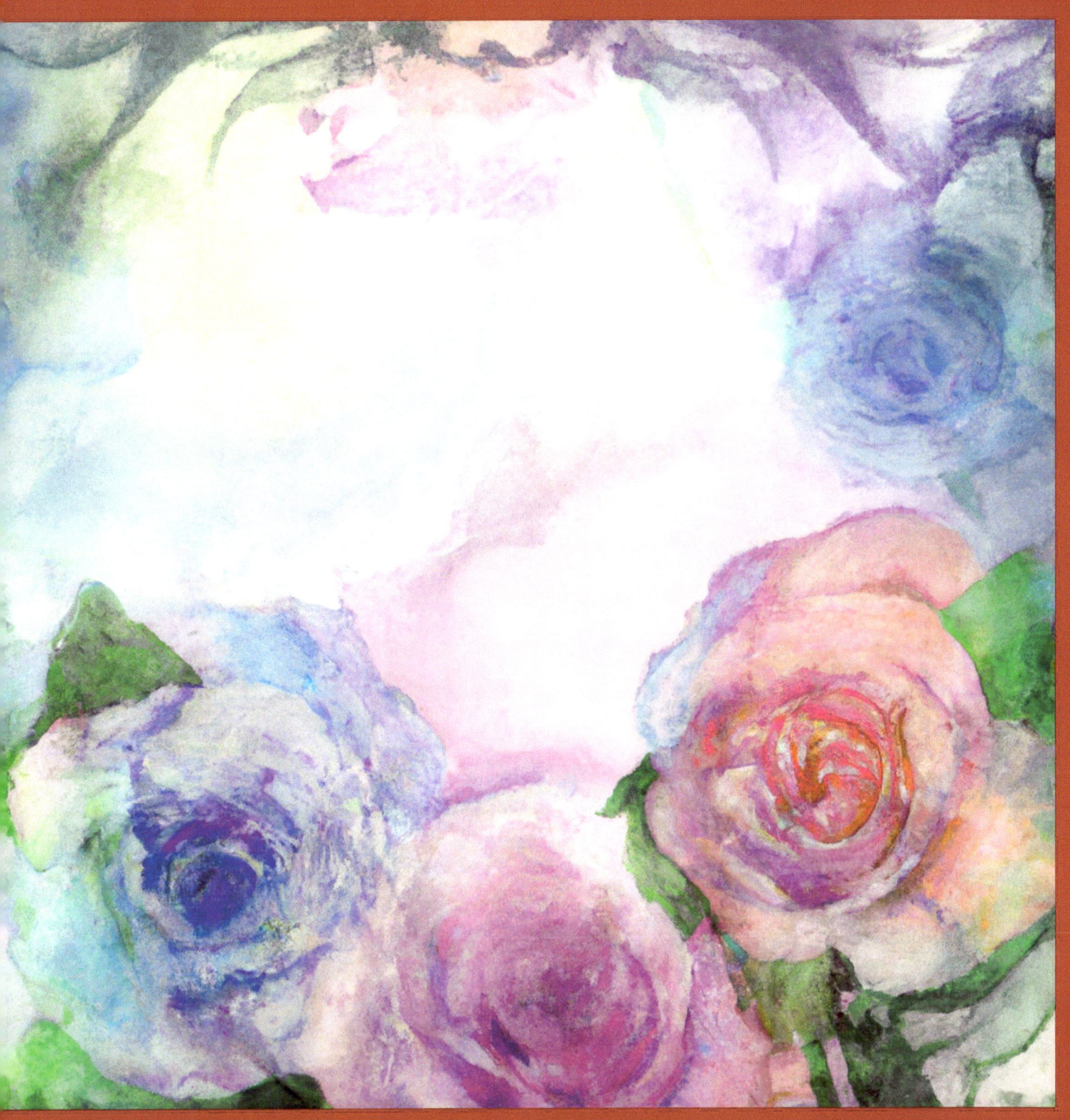

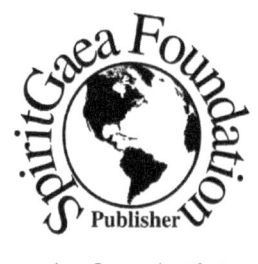

Author Artist

**Original Art
by Jeri Lee**

Copyright Jerilee.com
2022
All rights Reserved

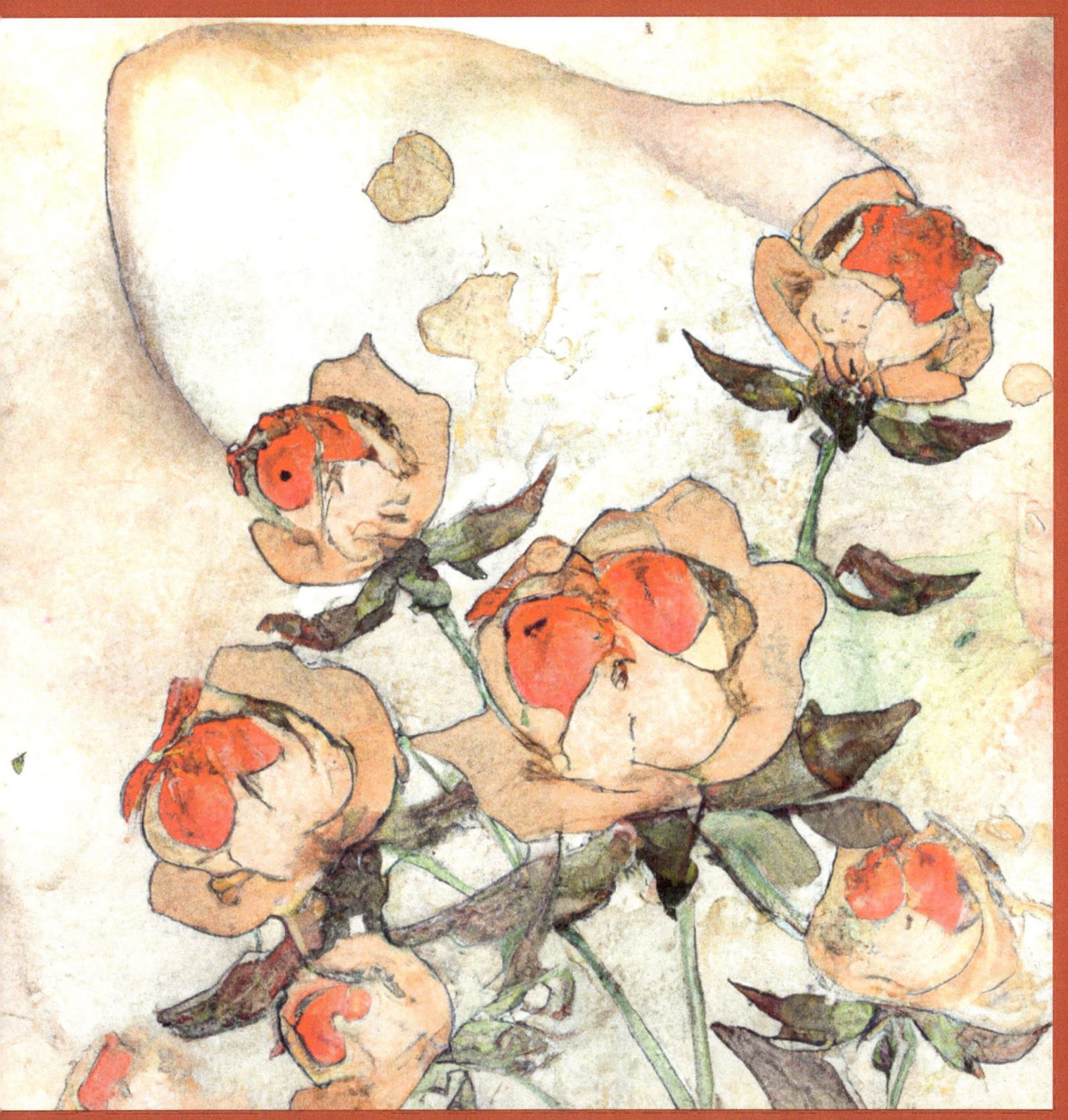

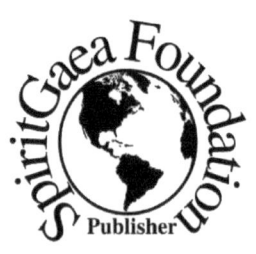

Author Artist

**Original Art
by Jeri Lee**

Copyright Jerilee.com
2022
All rights Reserved

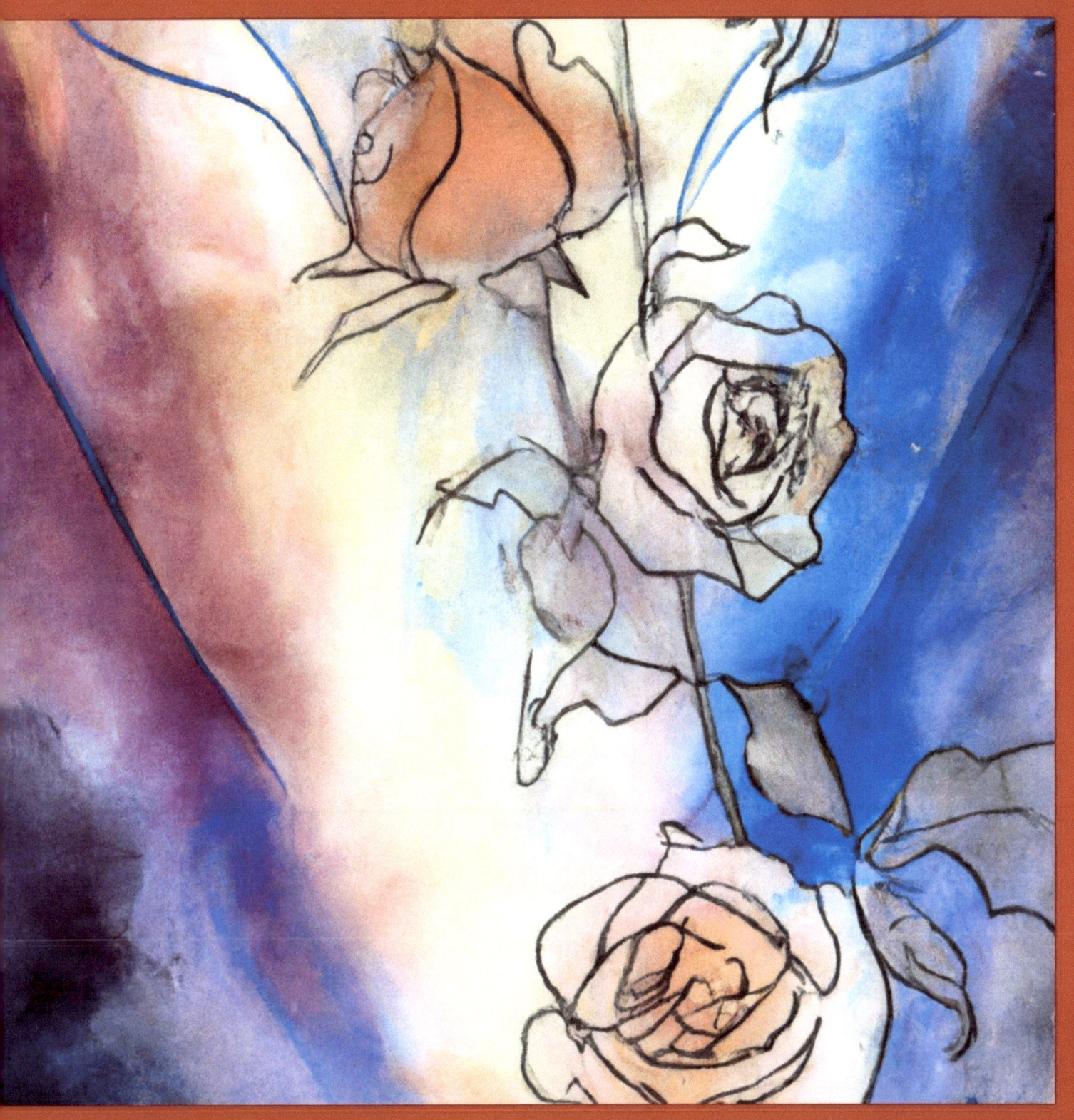

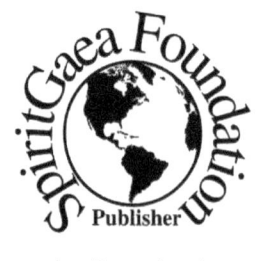

**Original Art
by Jeri Lee**

Copyright Jerilee.com
2022
All rights Reserved

Author Artist

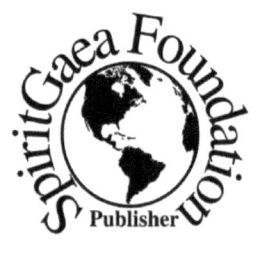

Author Artist

**Original Art
by Jeri Lee**

Copyright Jerilee.com
2022
All rights Reserved

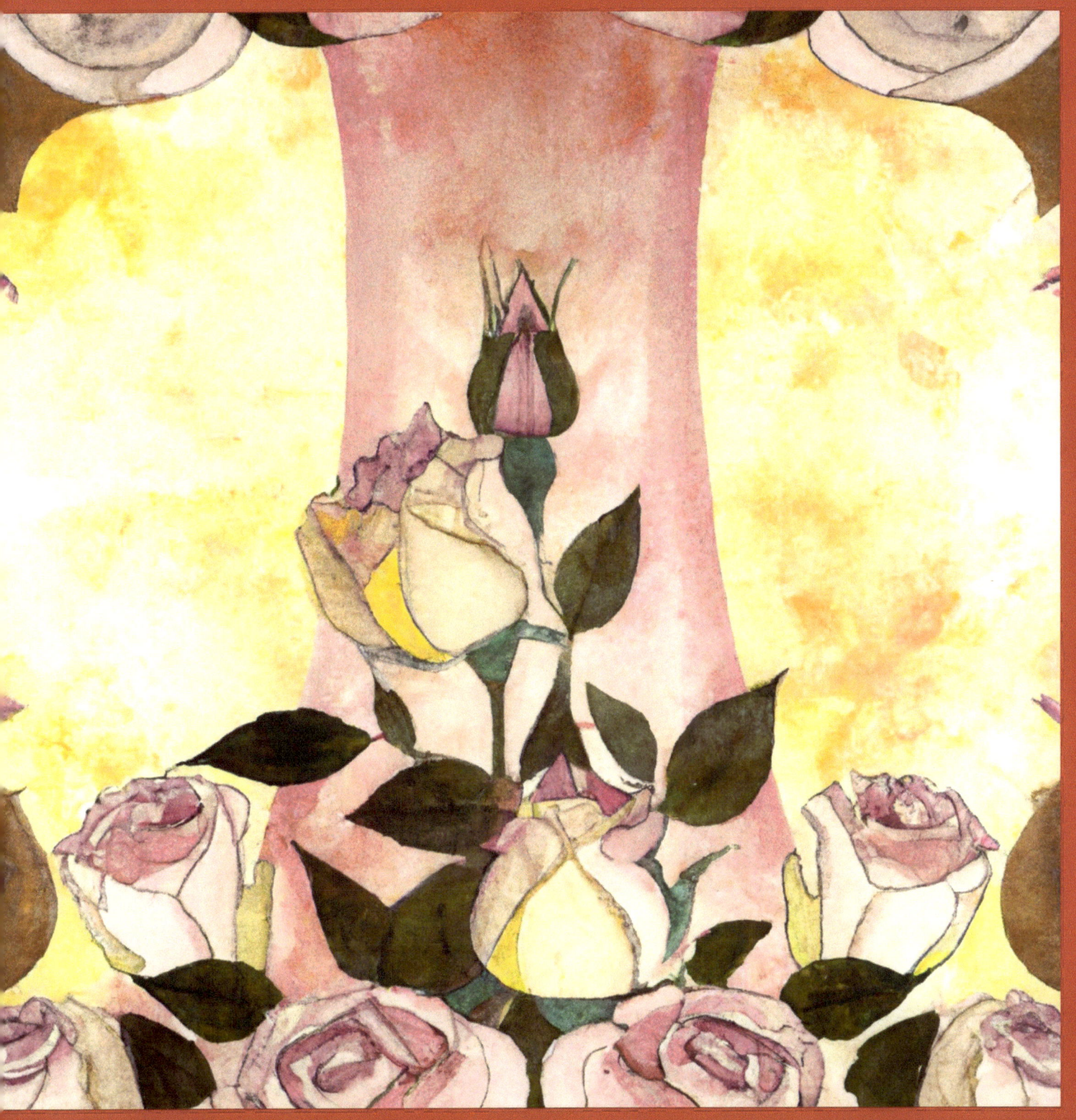

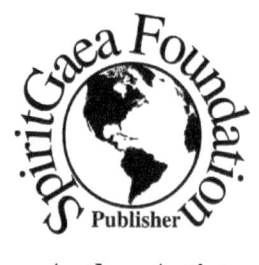

Original Art by Jeri Lee

Copyright Jerilee.com
2022
All rights Reserved

Author Artist

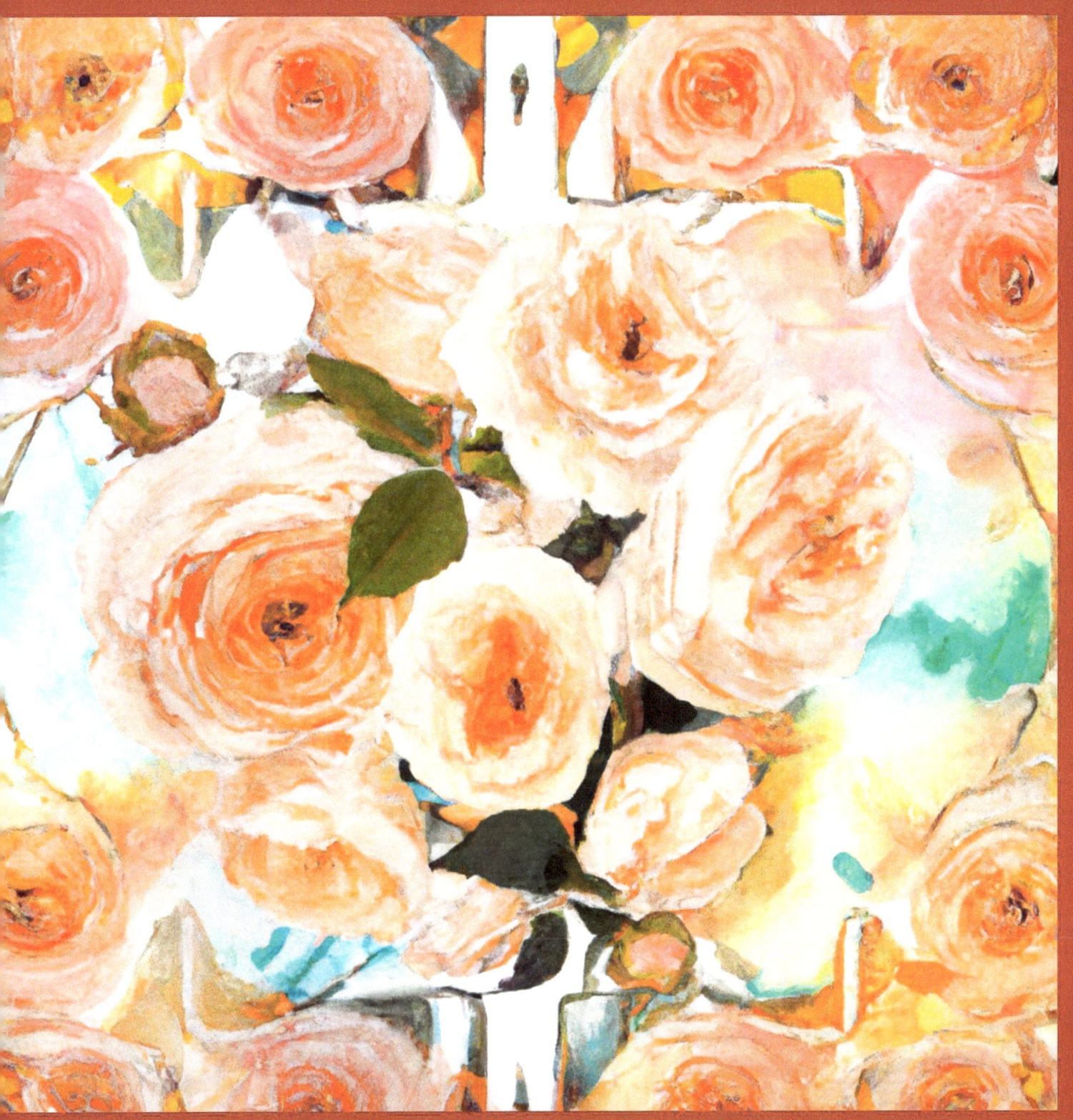

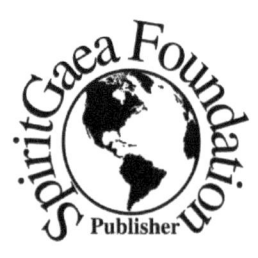

Author Artist

**Original Art
by Jeri Lee**

Copyright Jerilee.com
2022
All rights Reserved

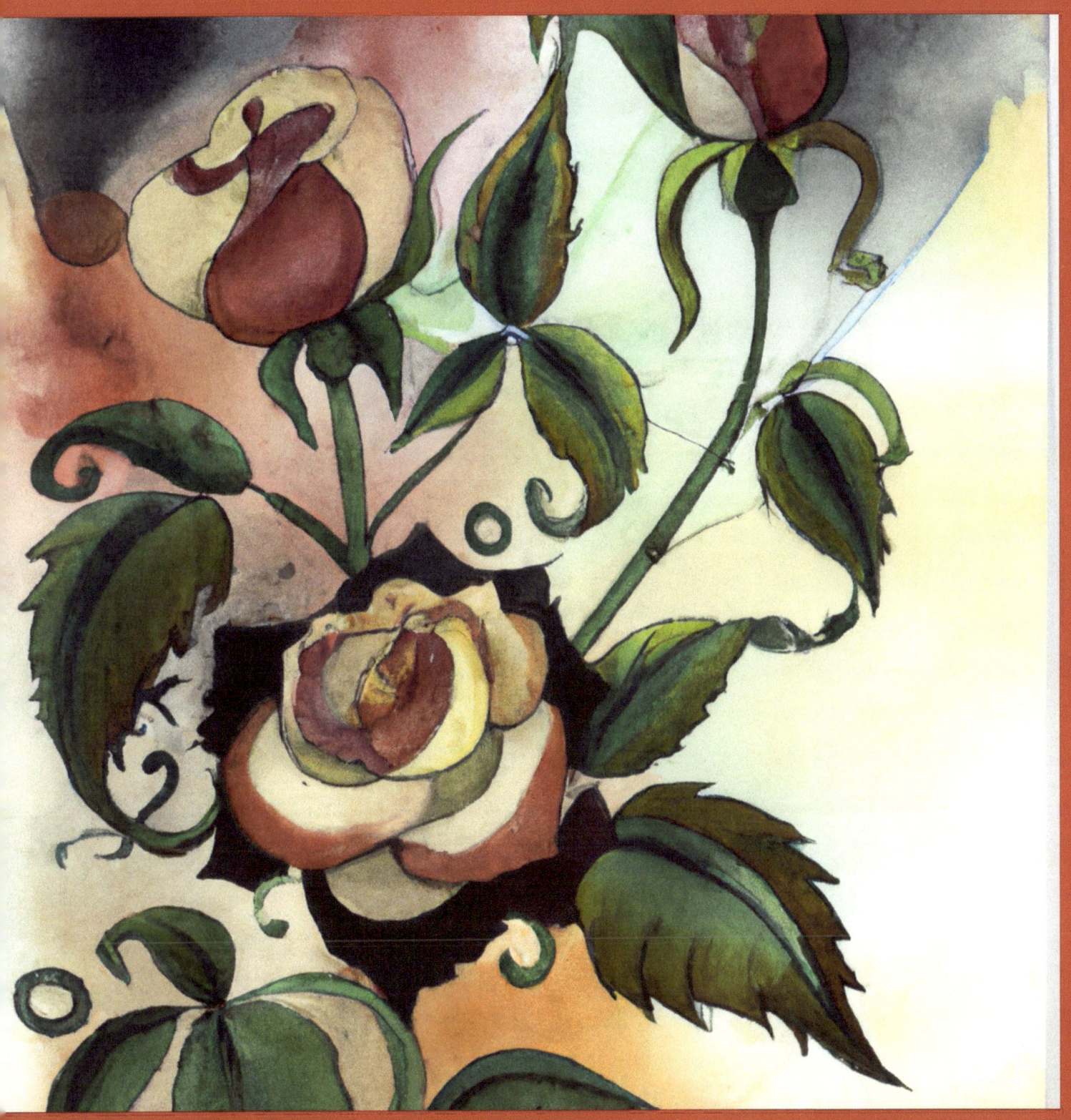

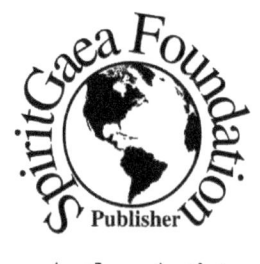

**Original Art
by Jeri Lee**

Copyright Jerilee.com
2022
All rights Reserved

Author Artist

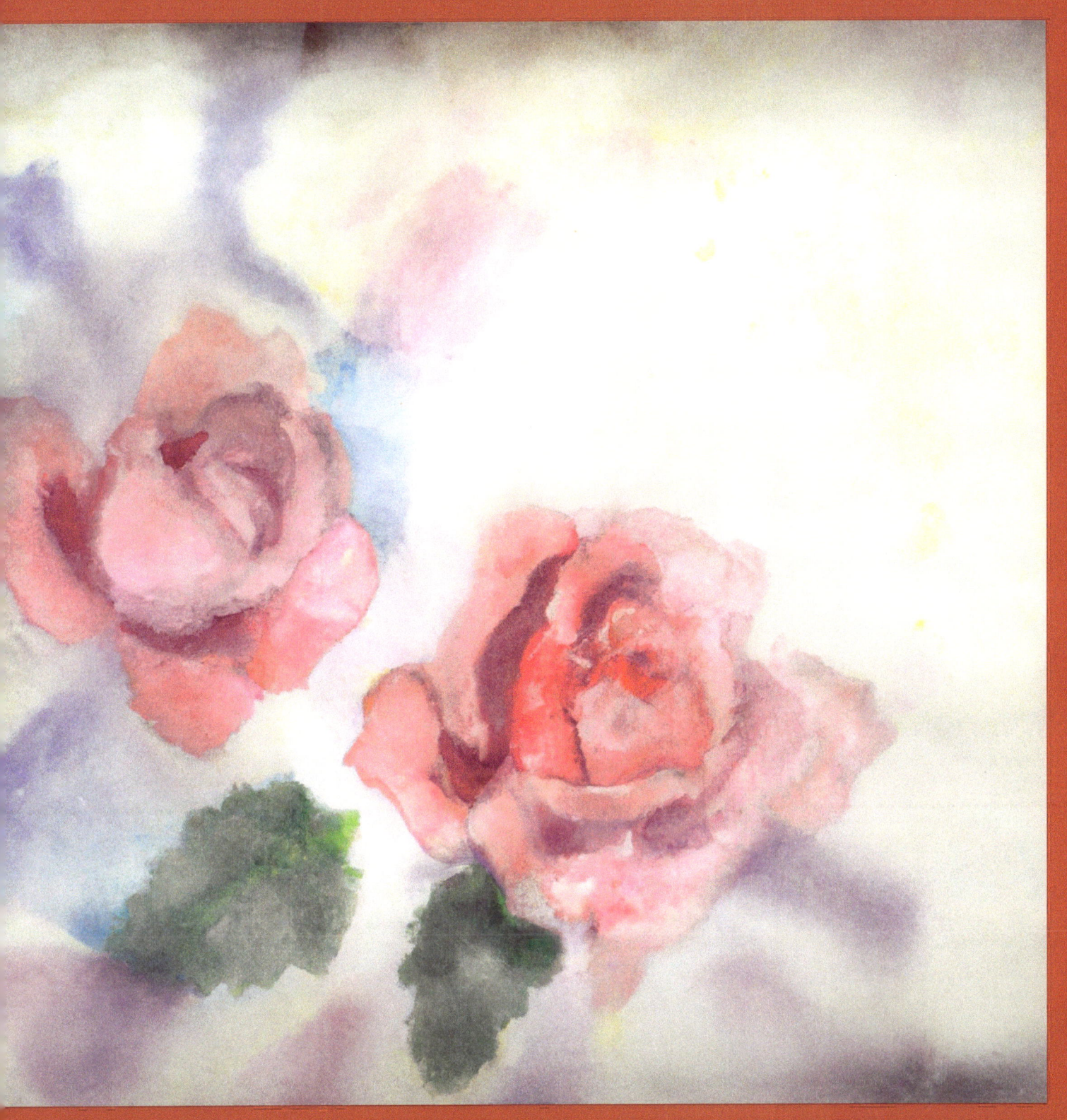

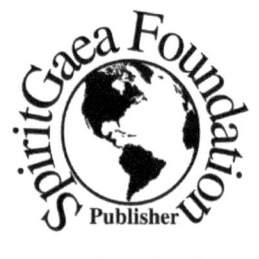

Original Art by Jeri Lee

Copyright Jerilee.com
2022
All rights Reserved

Author Artist

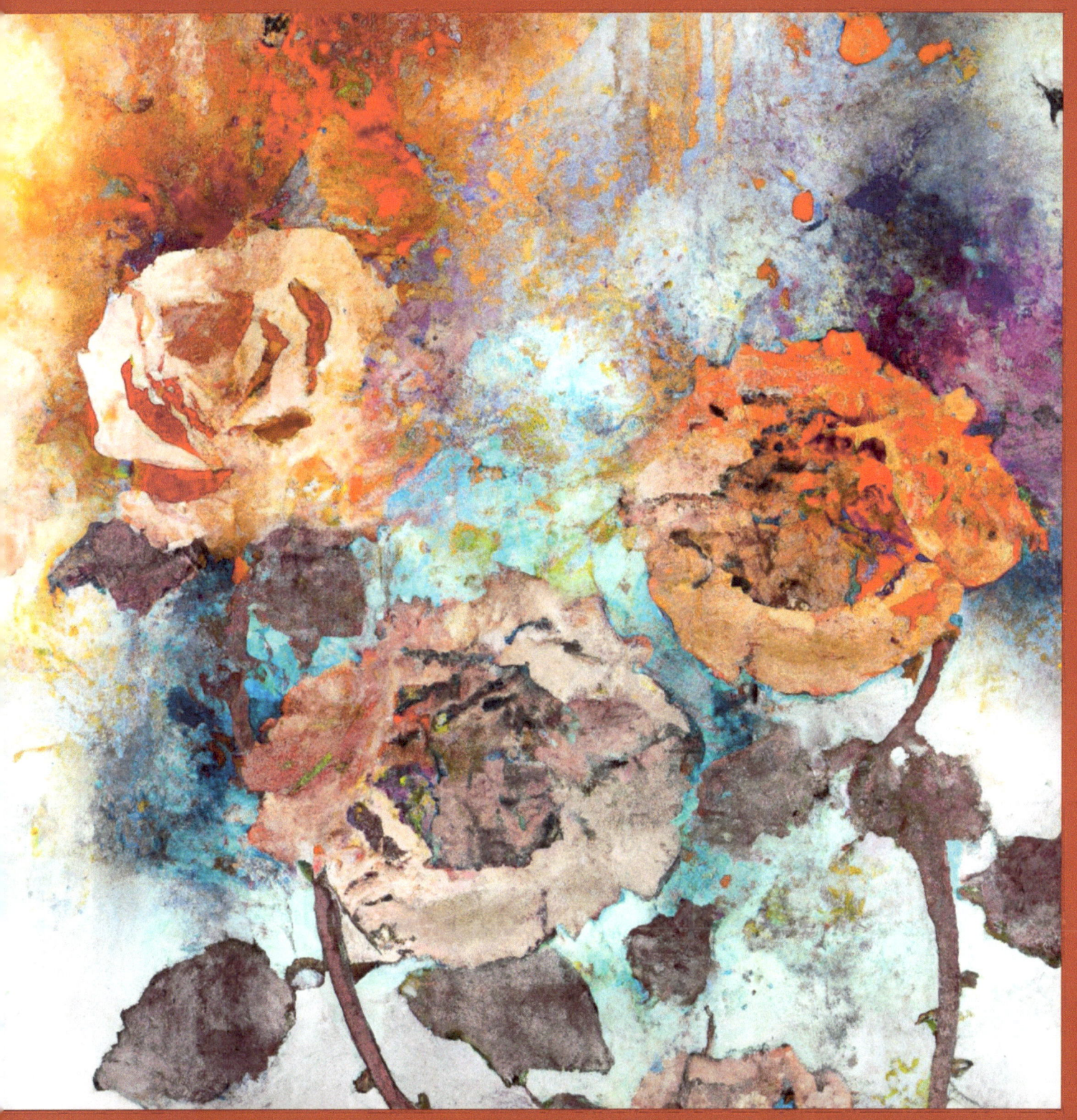

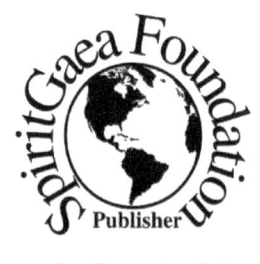

Author Artist

**Original Art
by Jeri Lee**

Copyright Jerilee.com
2022
All rights Reserved

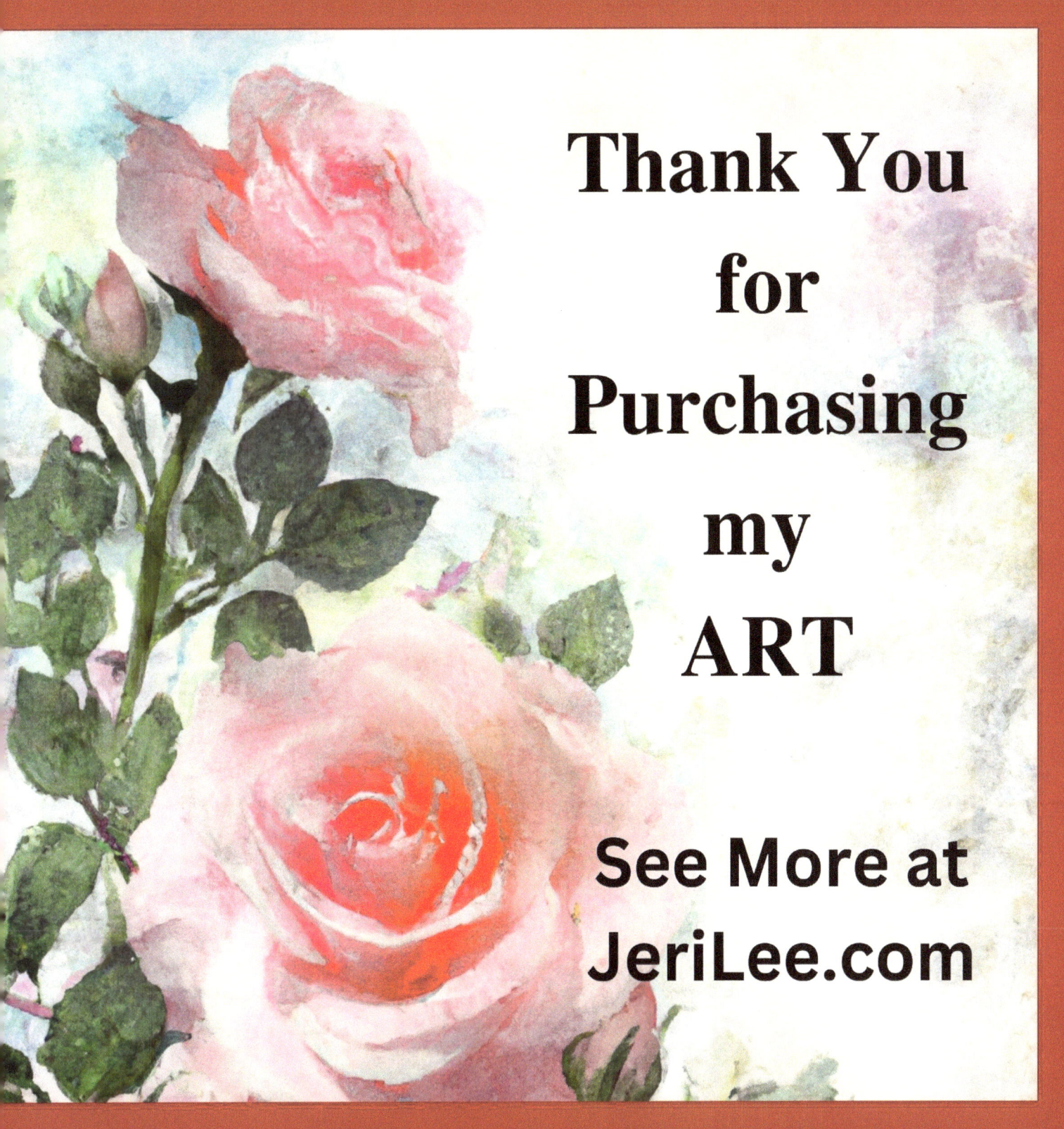

You Might enjoy one of my many coloring books, Most of which are designed with Adults in mind.

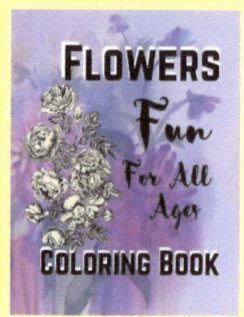
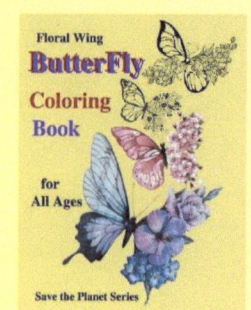
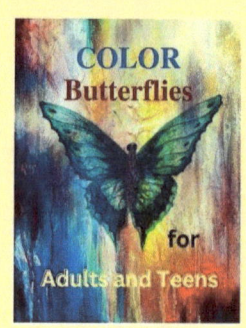
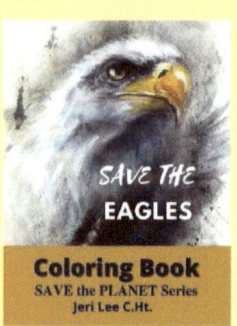
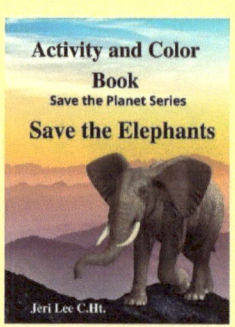
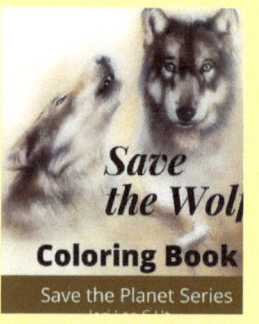
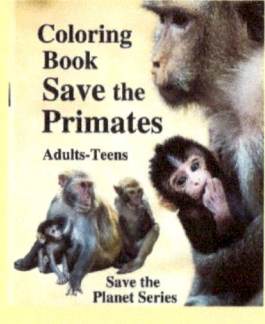
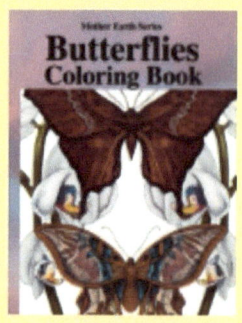
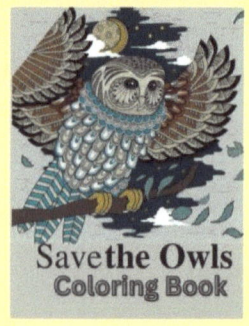
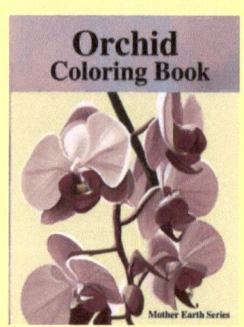
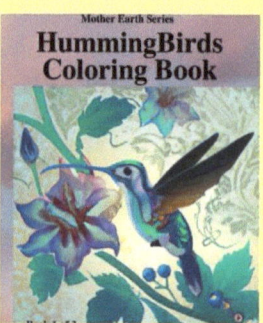
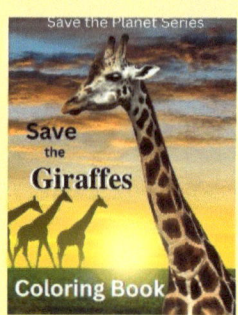
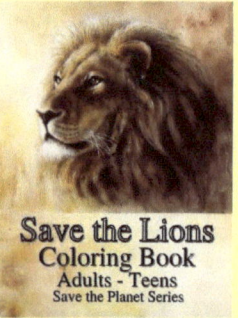

My Coloring books are 8.5 x 11 with 50 to 100 pages to color. They are focused on Save the Planet and pages can be view on my website. www,jerilee.com   purchases on Amazon.com

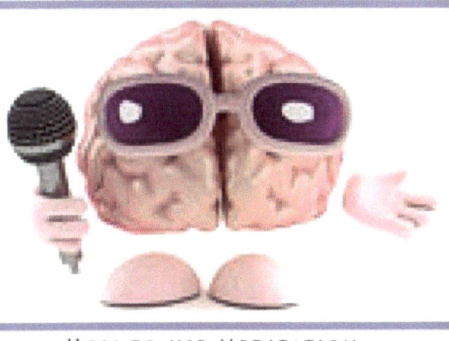

About the Artist-Author

I was born in 1939 with an overactive ambition that even death could not alter. I have died twice but refuse to stay dead. I wrote Singiiing in the brain as a self-help book to share what I do to stay alive even in my 80s. From early life, pushing a pen or a brush has been my way of life.

Singing in the Brain

By using Meditation, Visualization and Self-Hypnosis you can sing yourself healthy. You utilize your right brain functions when you sing. Your voice is your best friend and is your natural tranquilizer so stay happy and healthy by singing to yourself. This is the true story of Author Jeri Lee, showing how she developed this process. This is a do it yourself book on finding your fountain of youth

Please Check out some of my other Prints

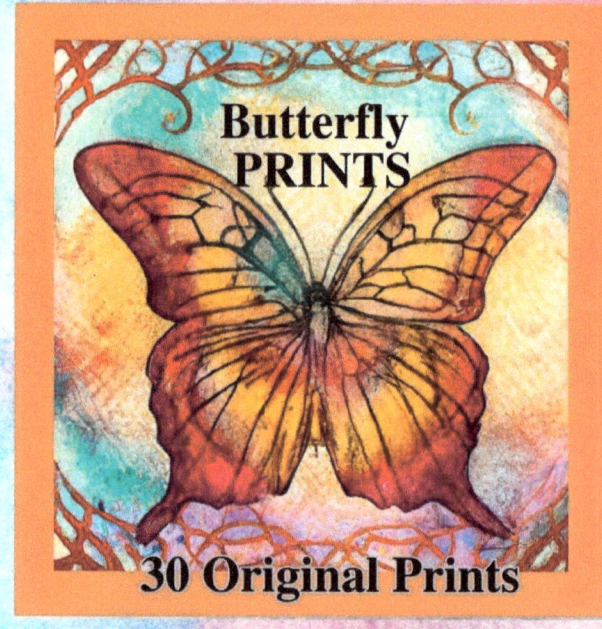
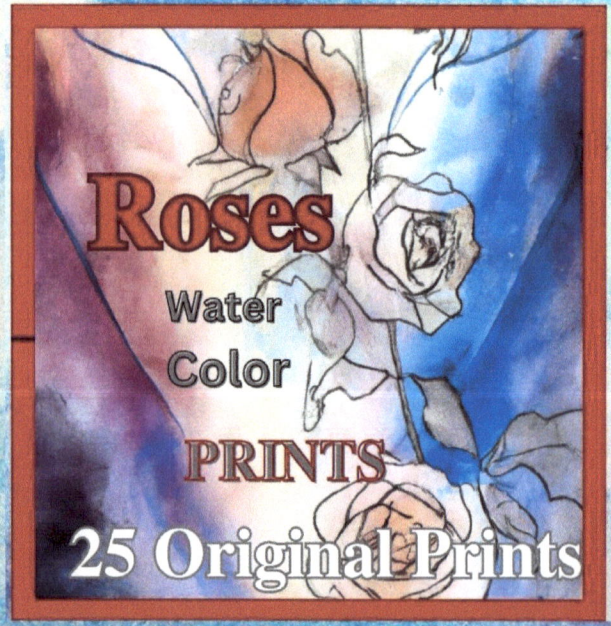
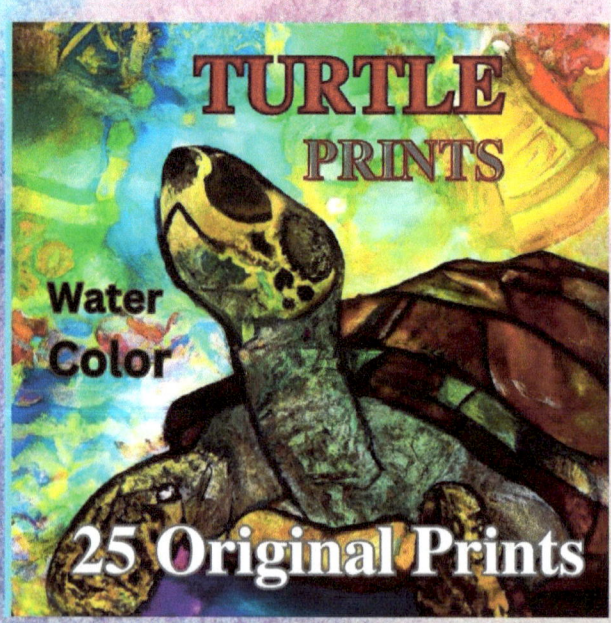

www.ingramcontent.com/pod-product-compliance
Lightning Source LLC
Chambersburg PA
CBHW041933240526
45473CB00034B/996

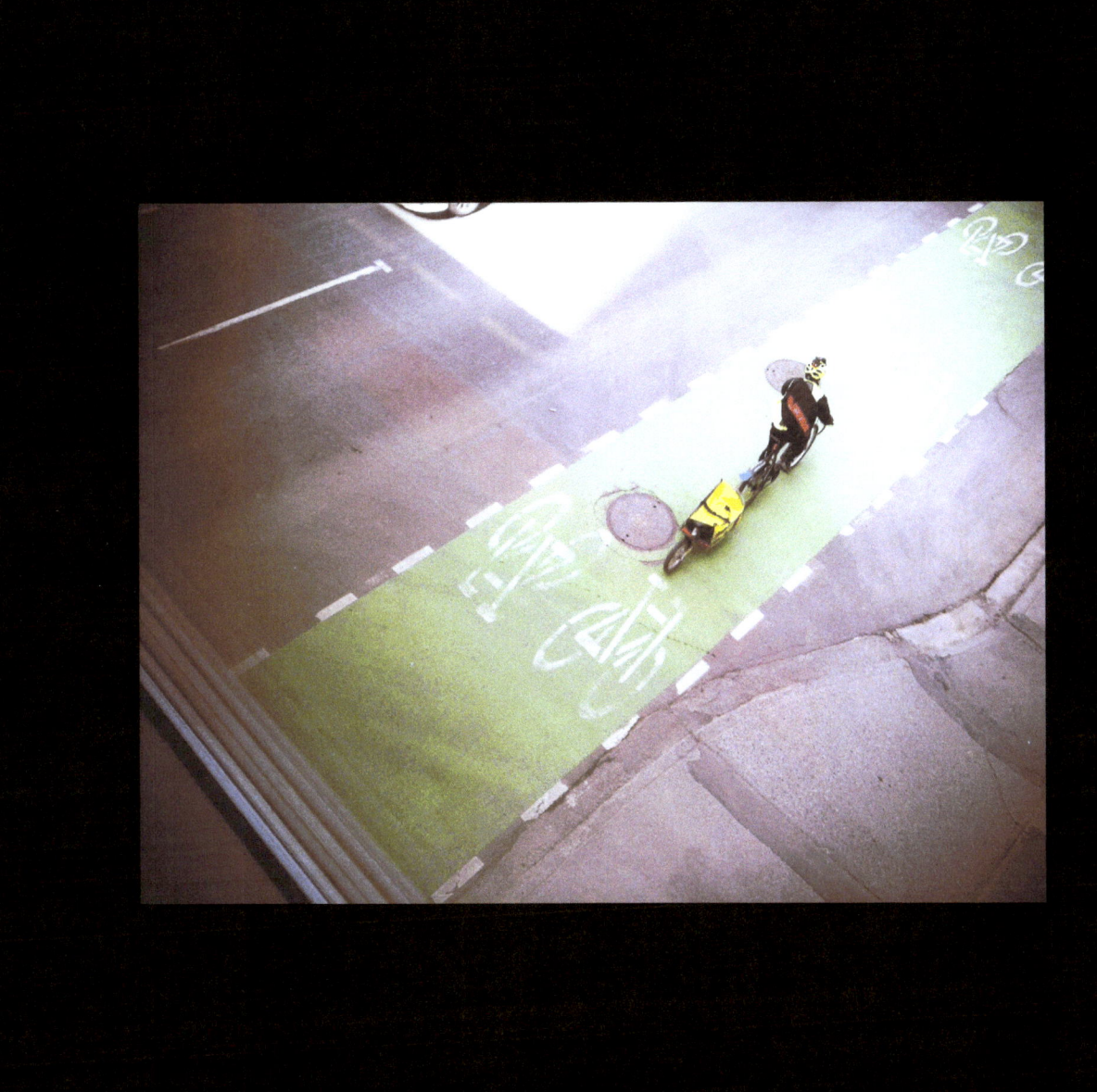

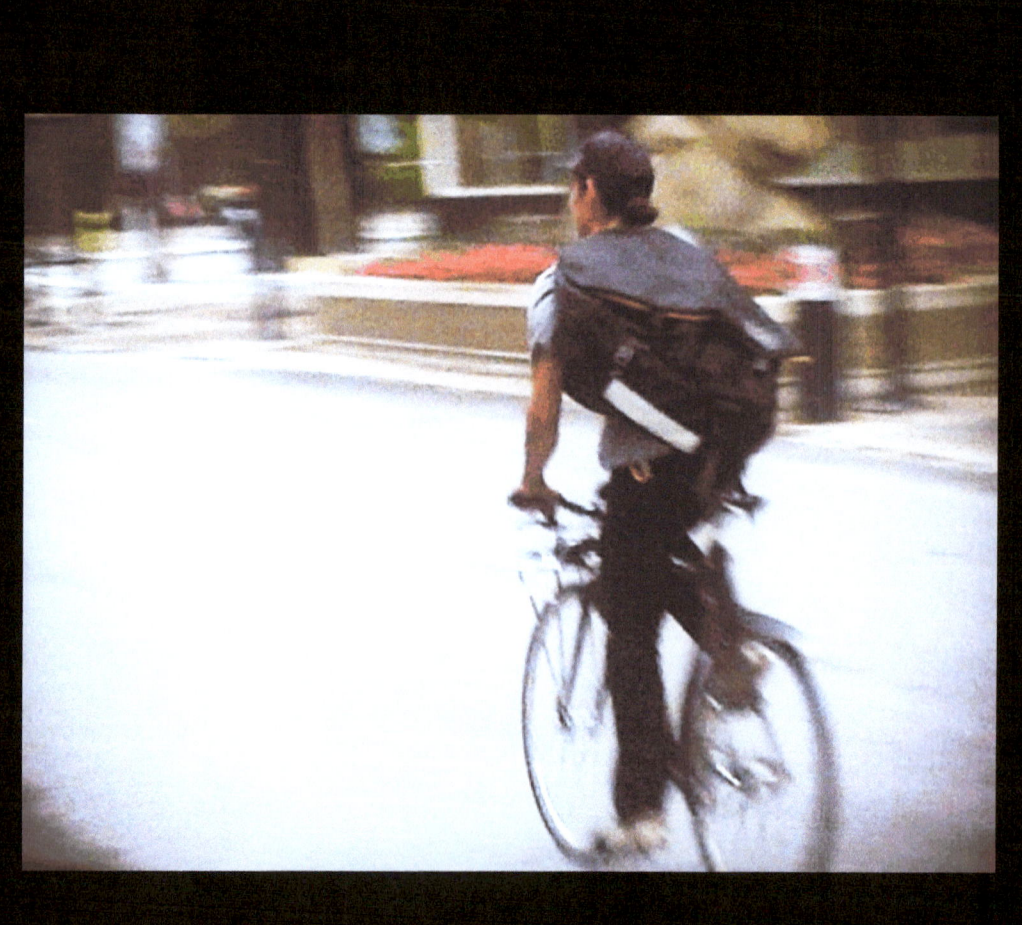

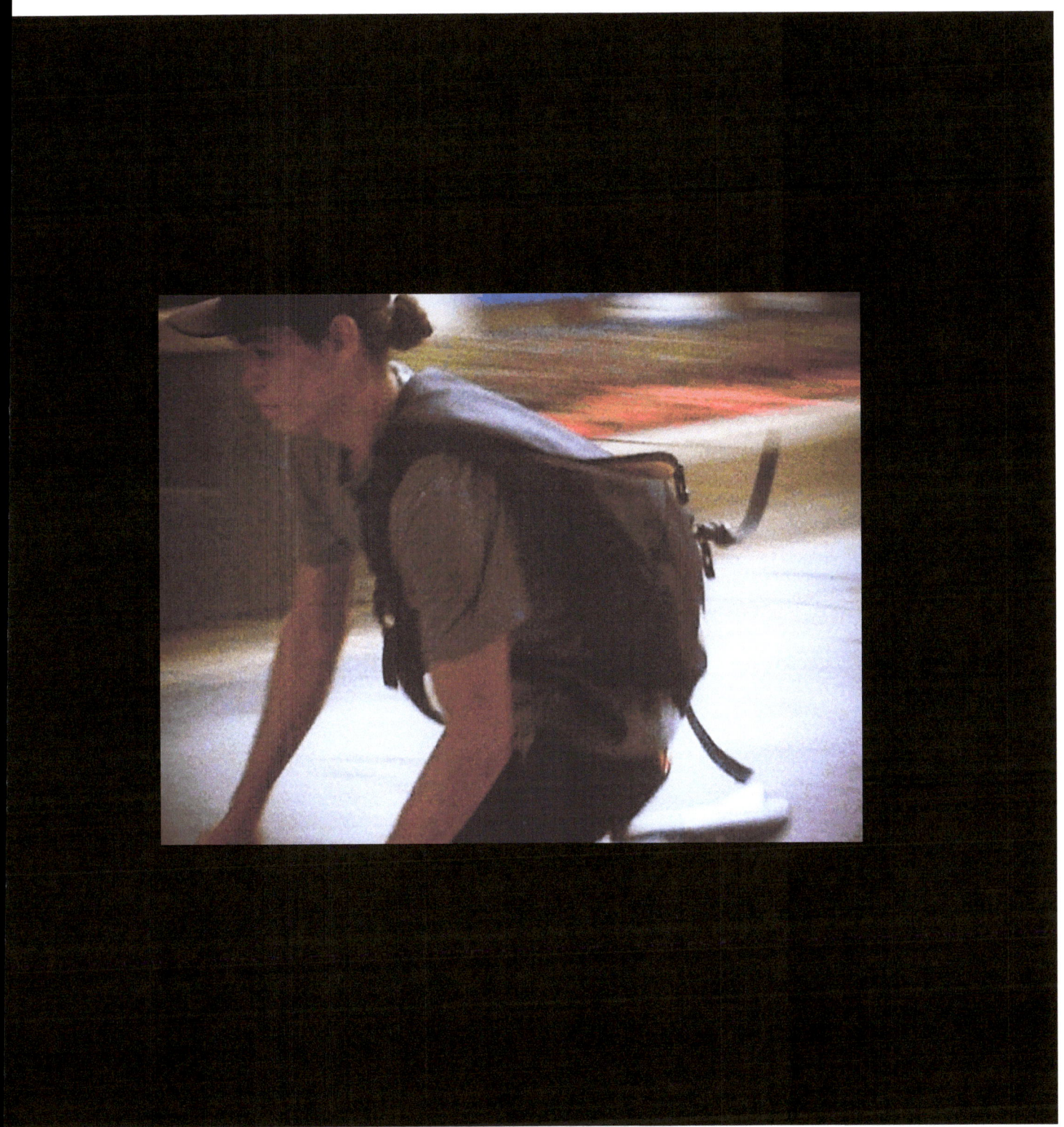

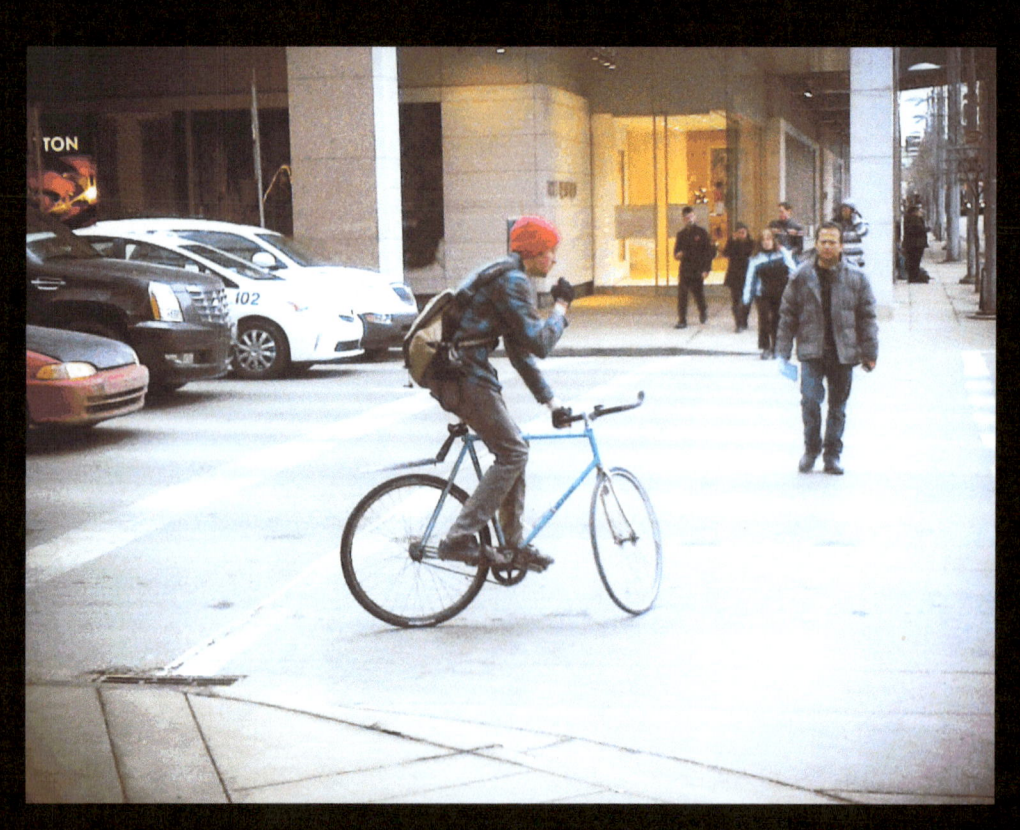

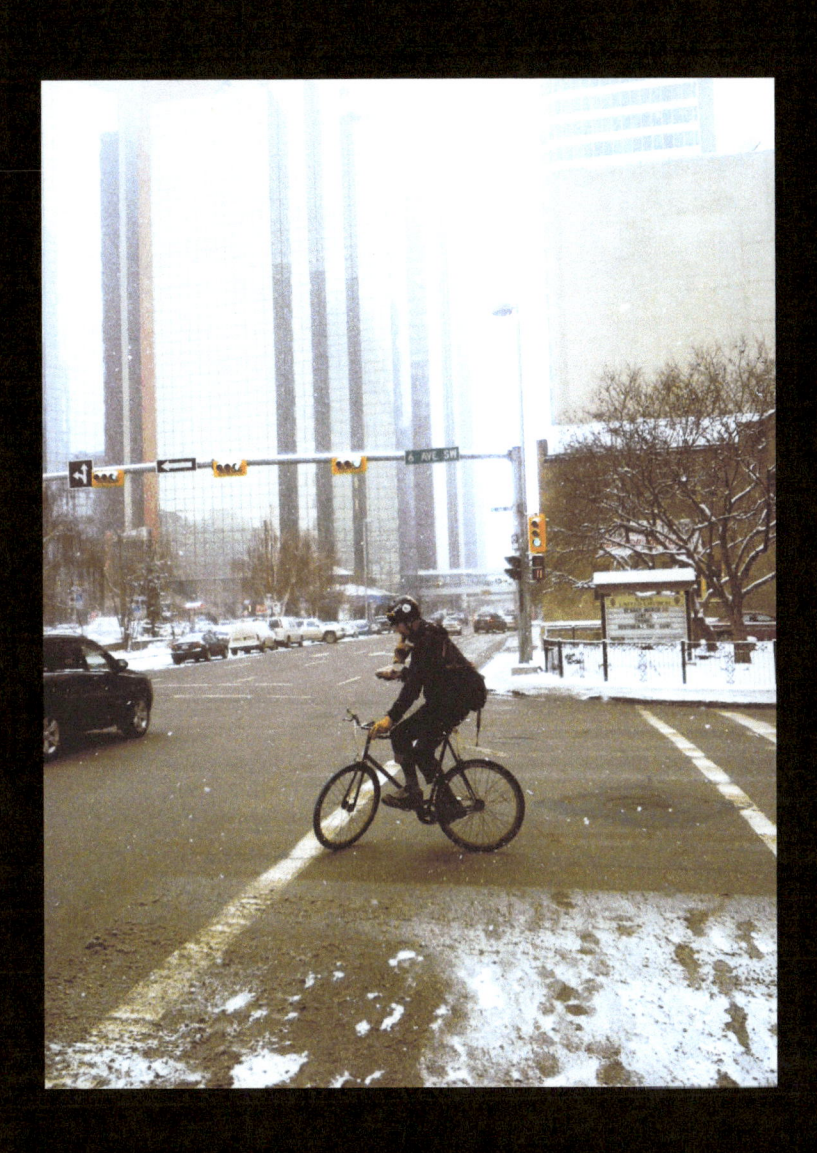

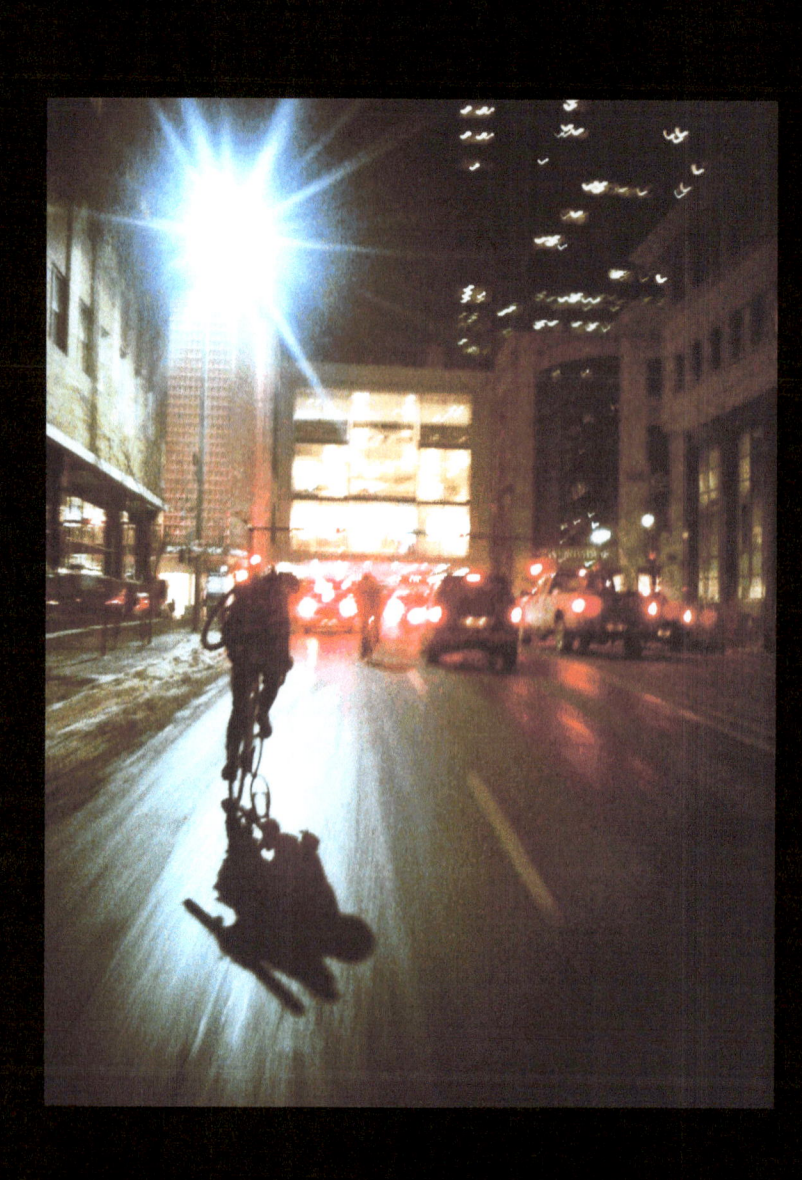

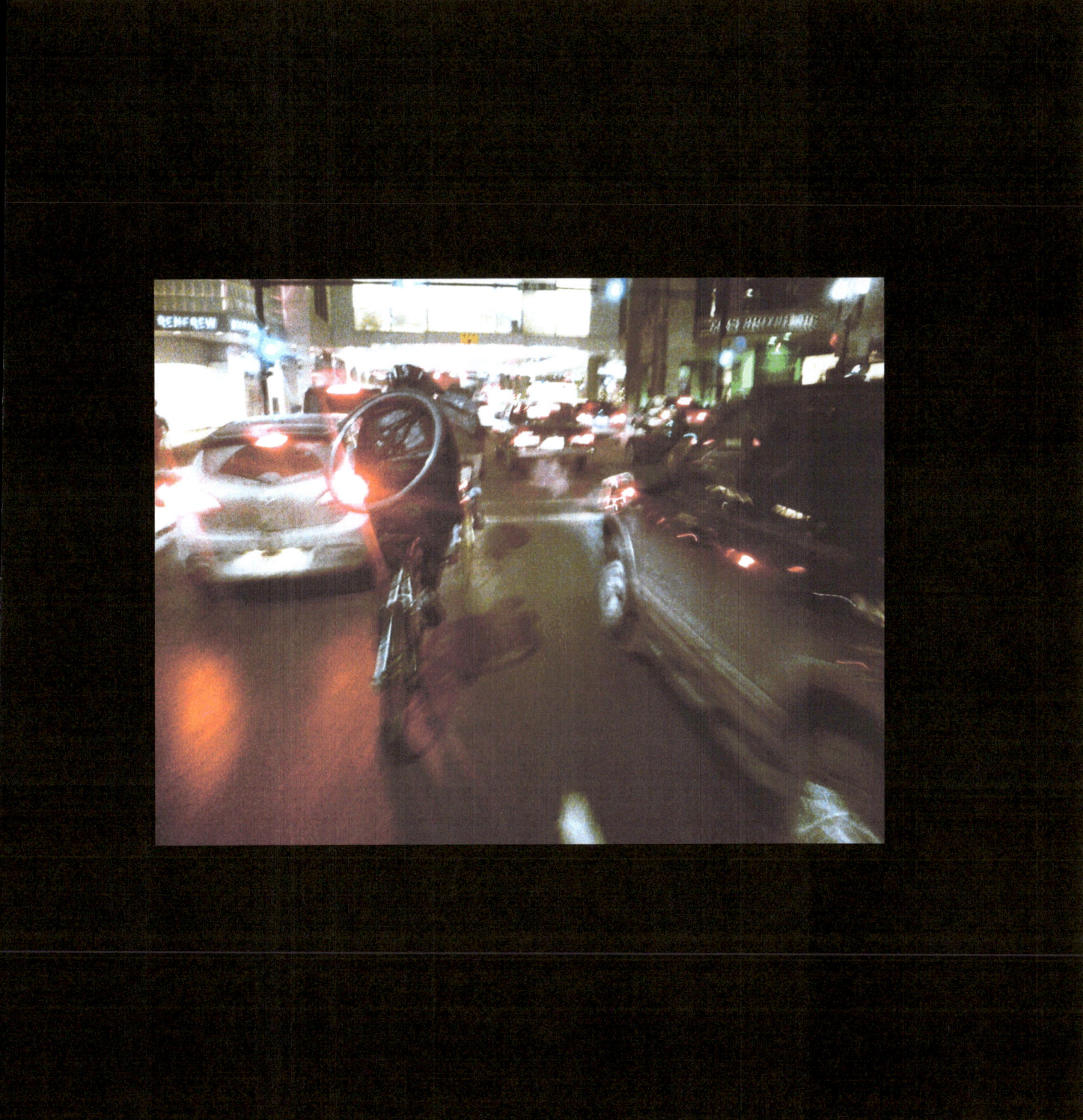

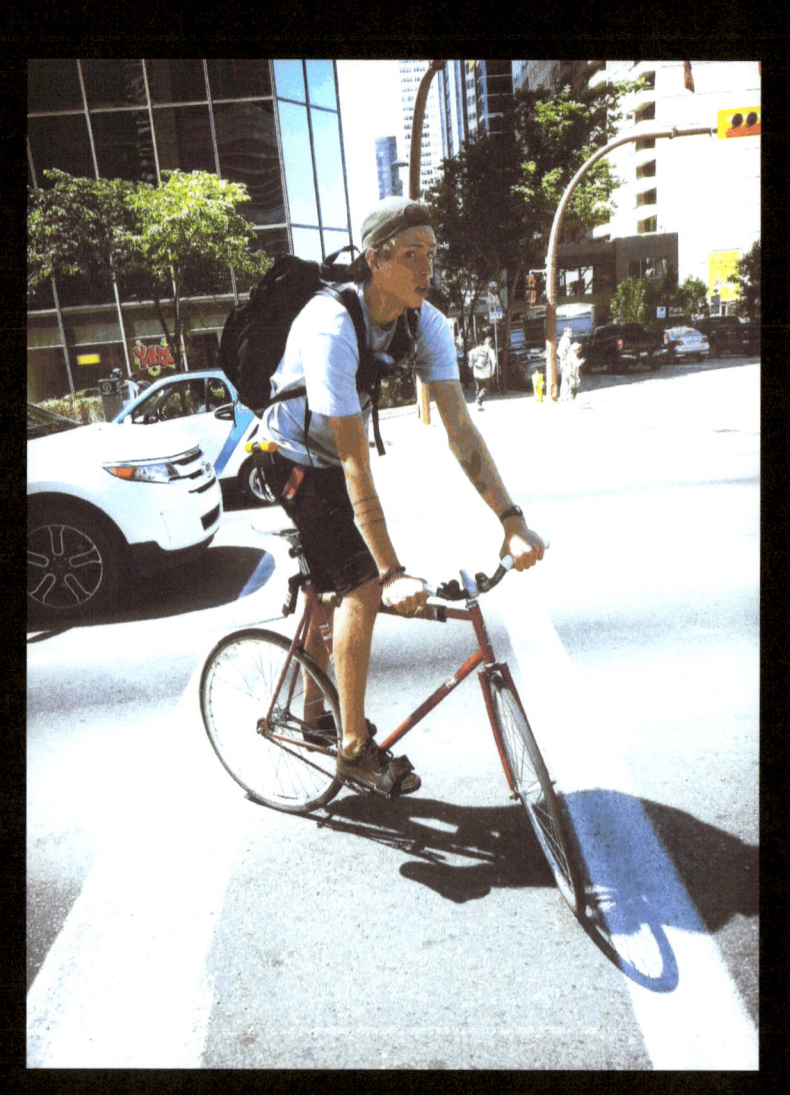

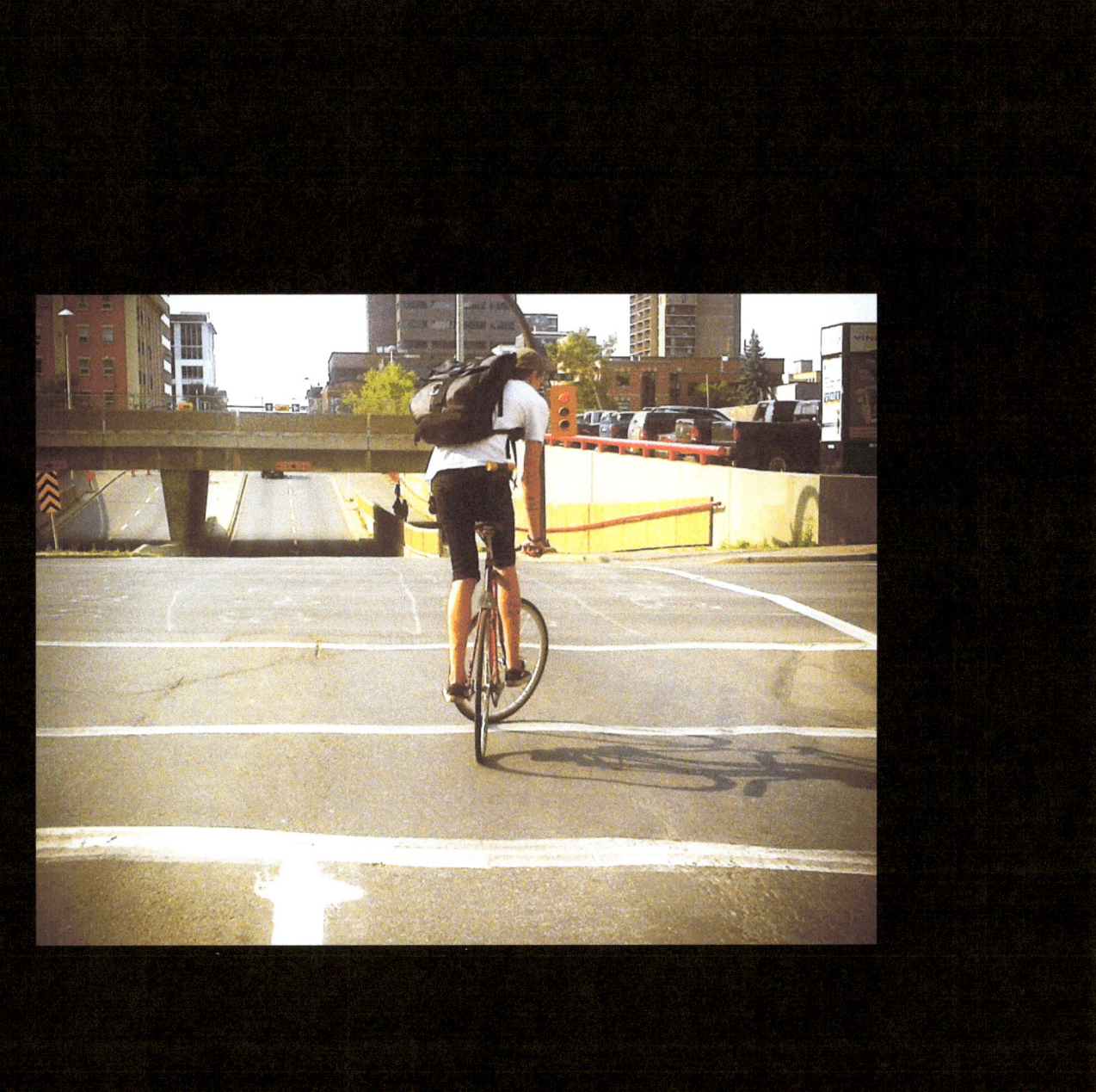

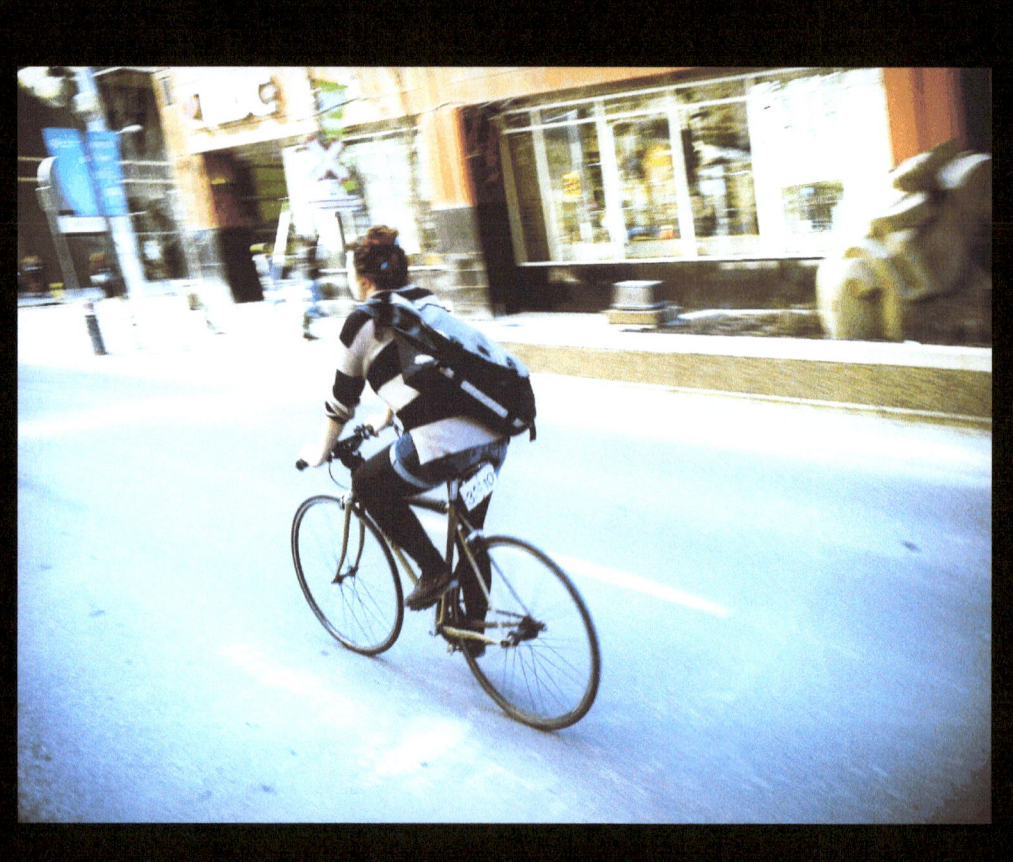

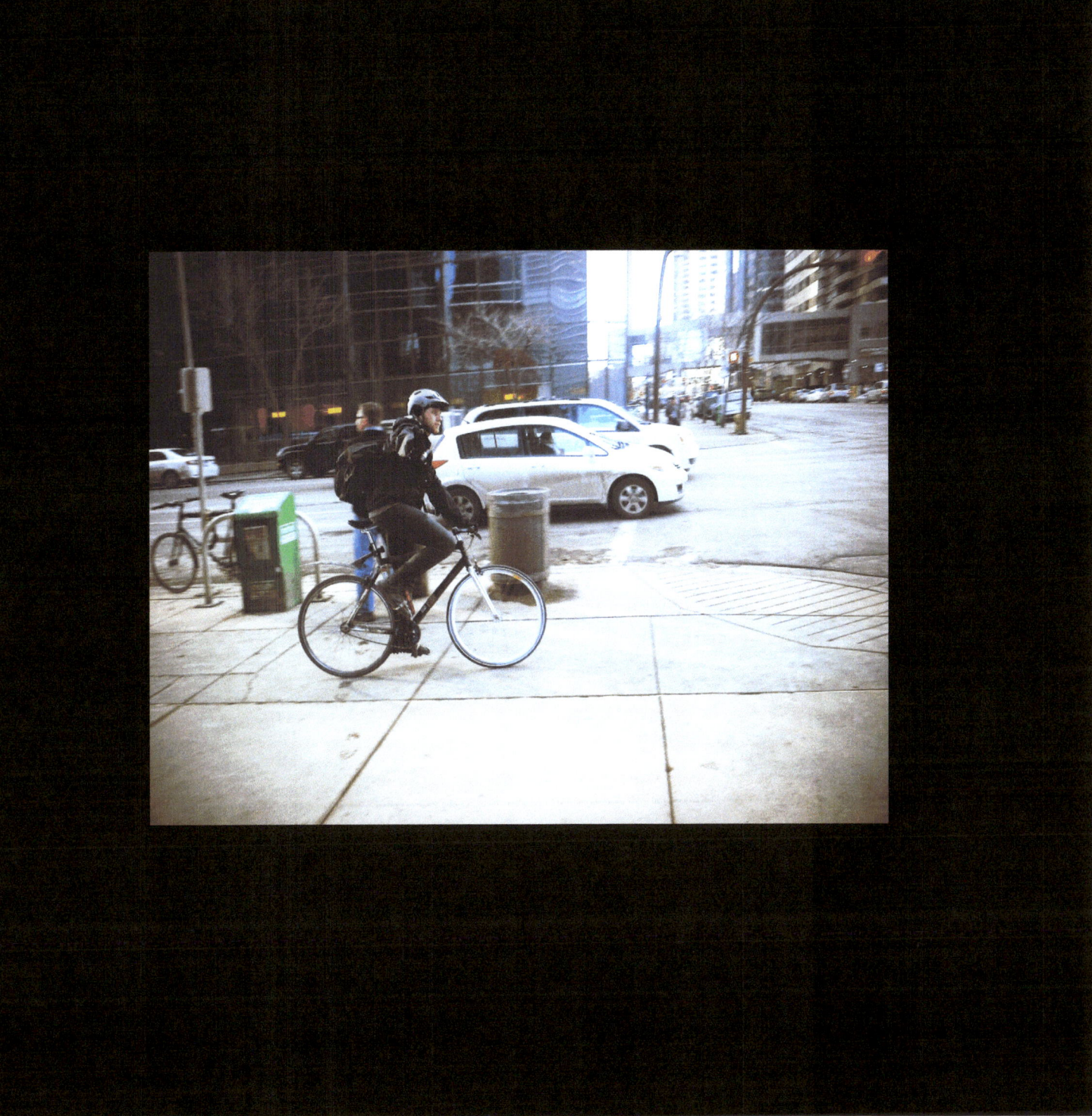

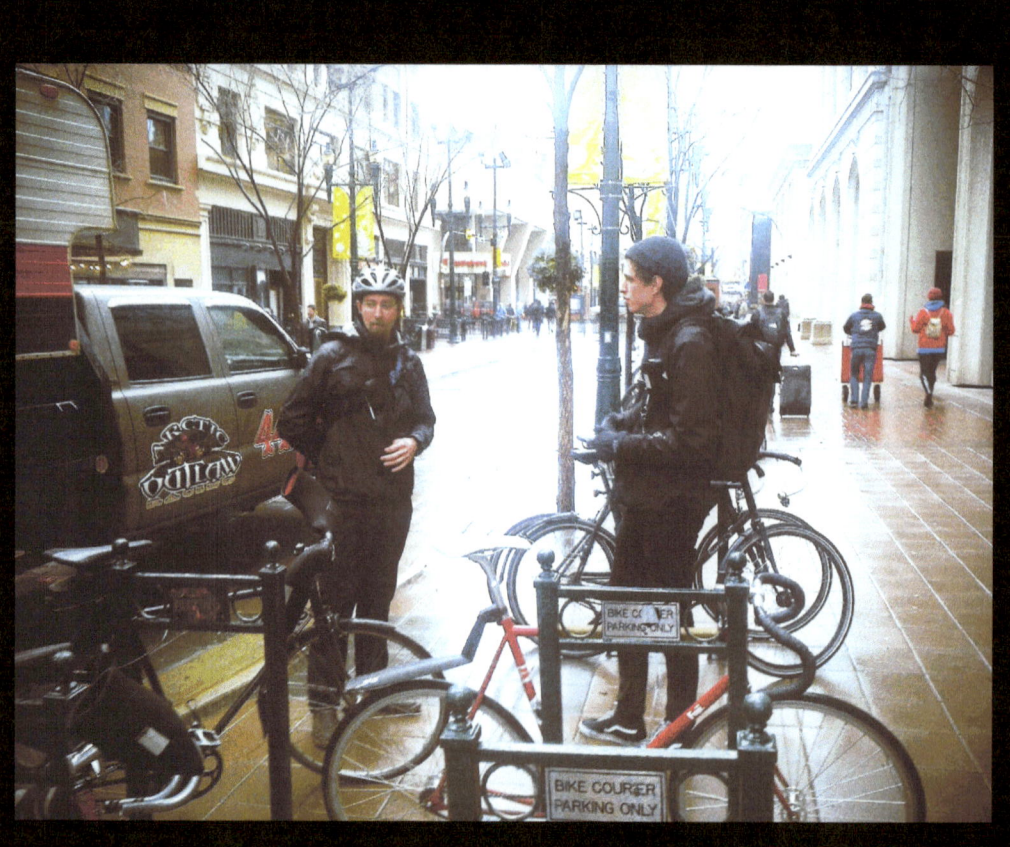

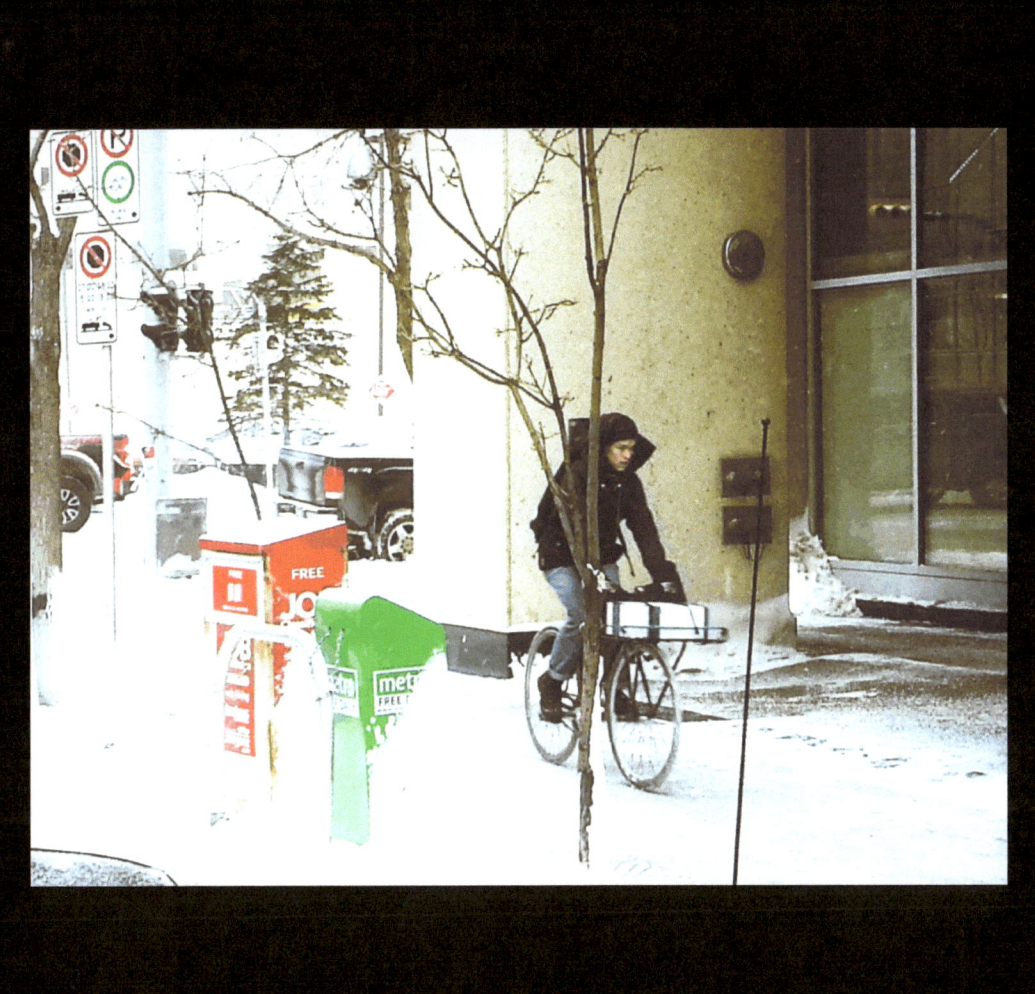

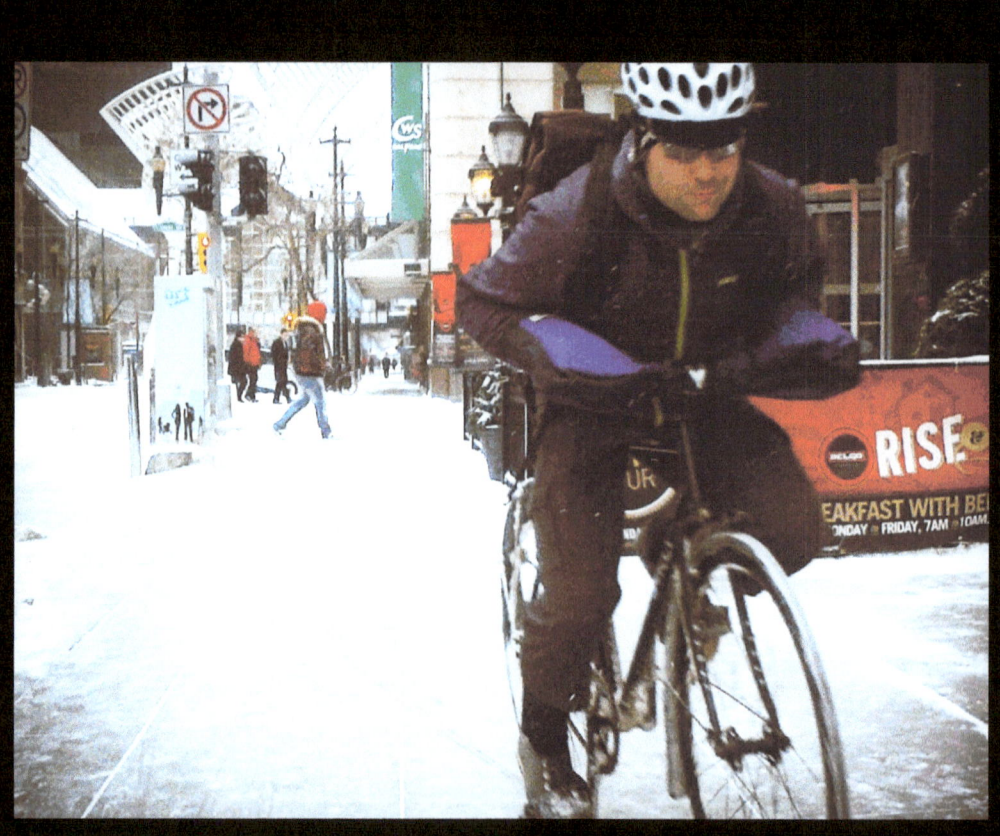

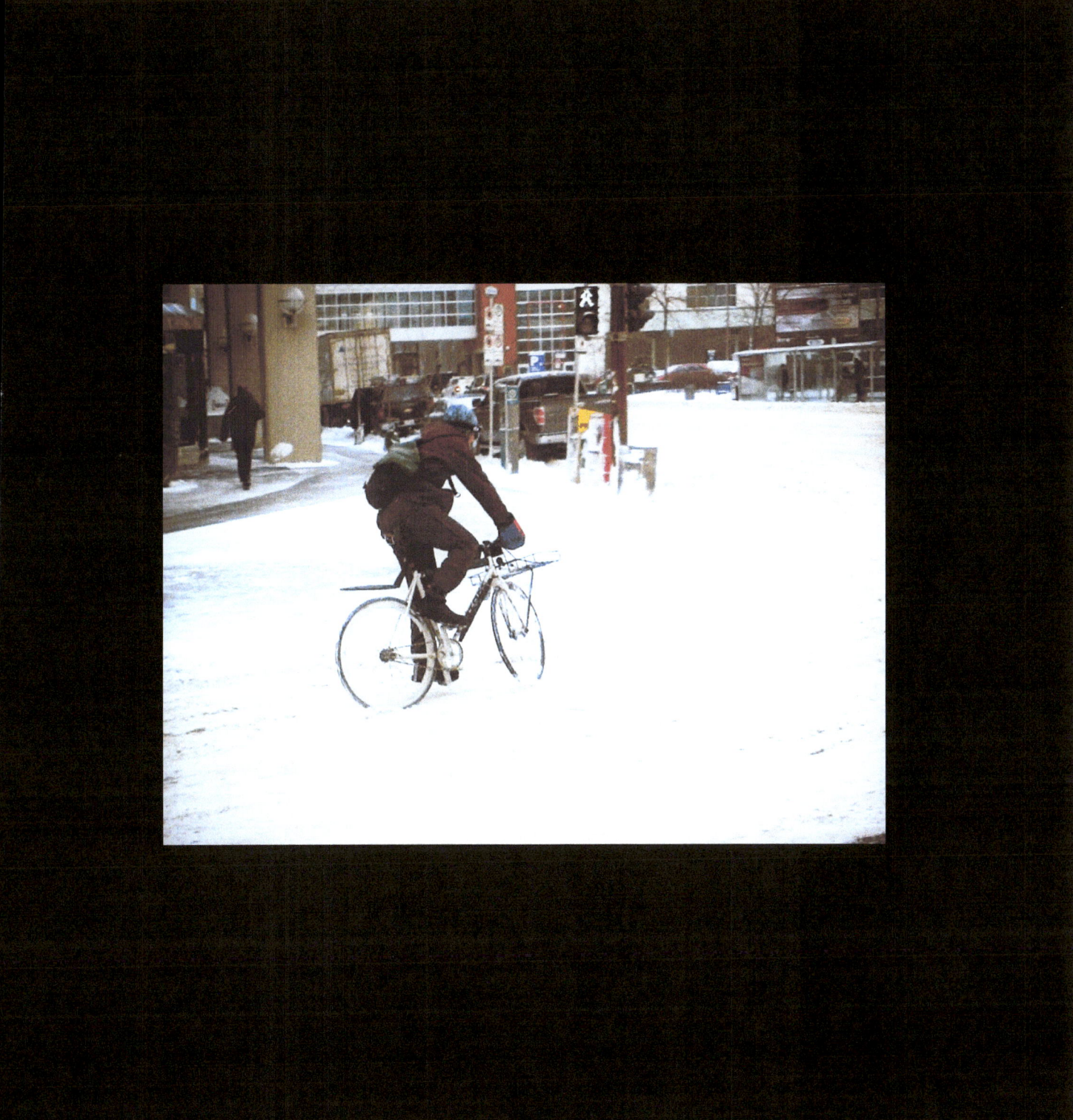

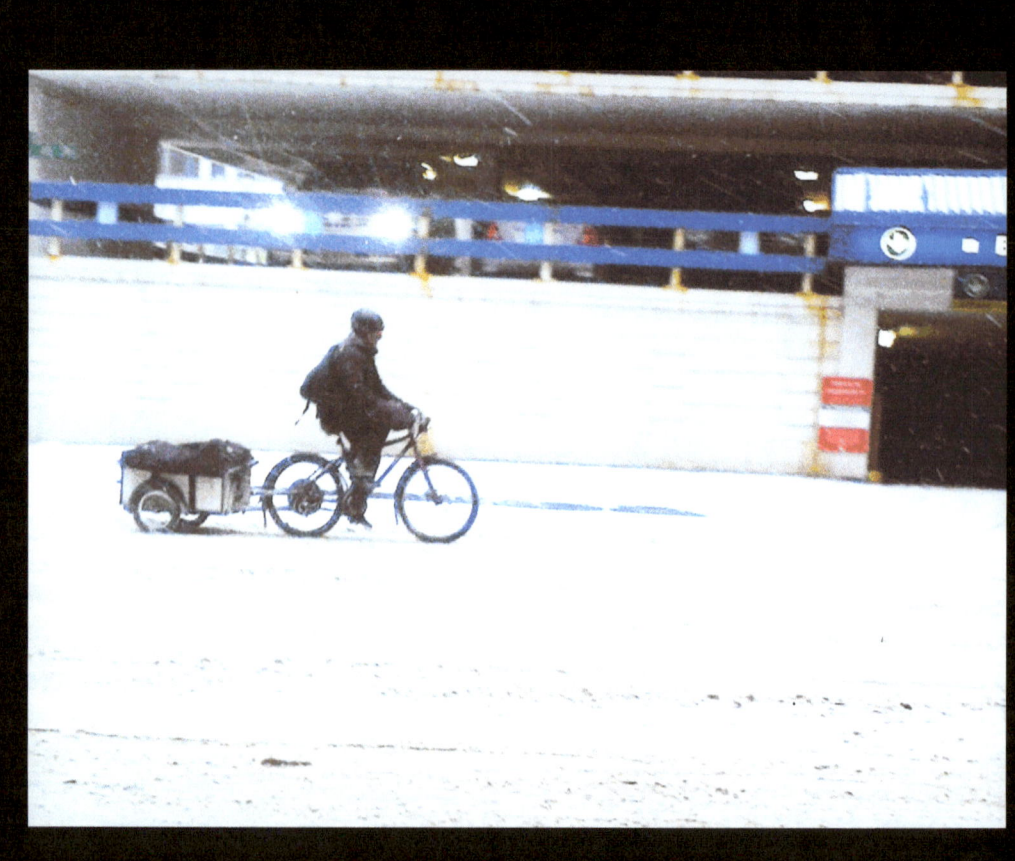

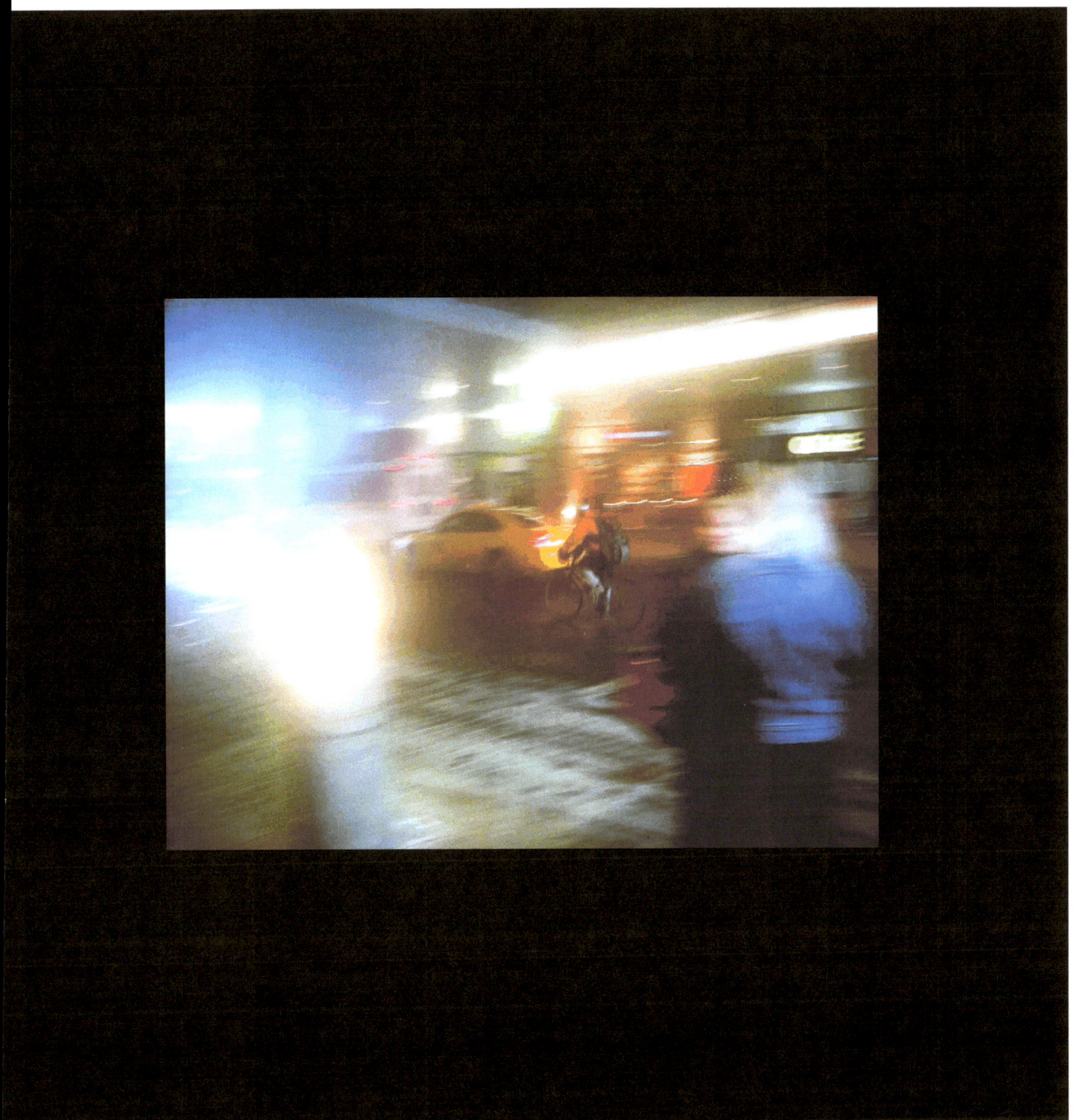

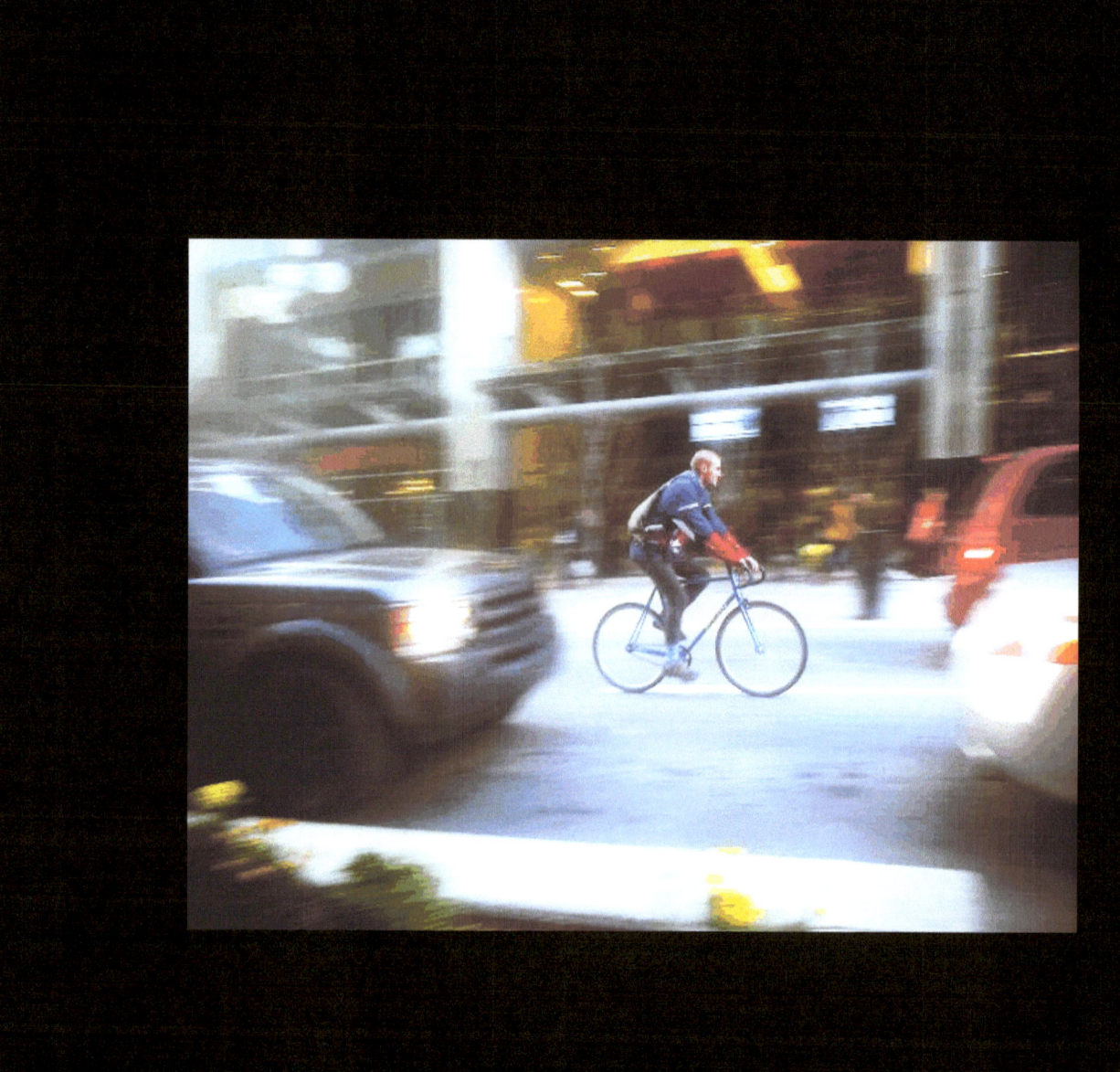

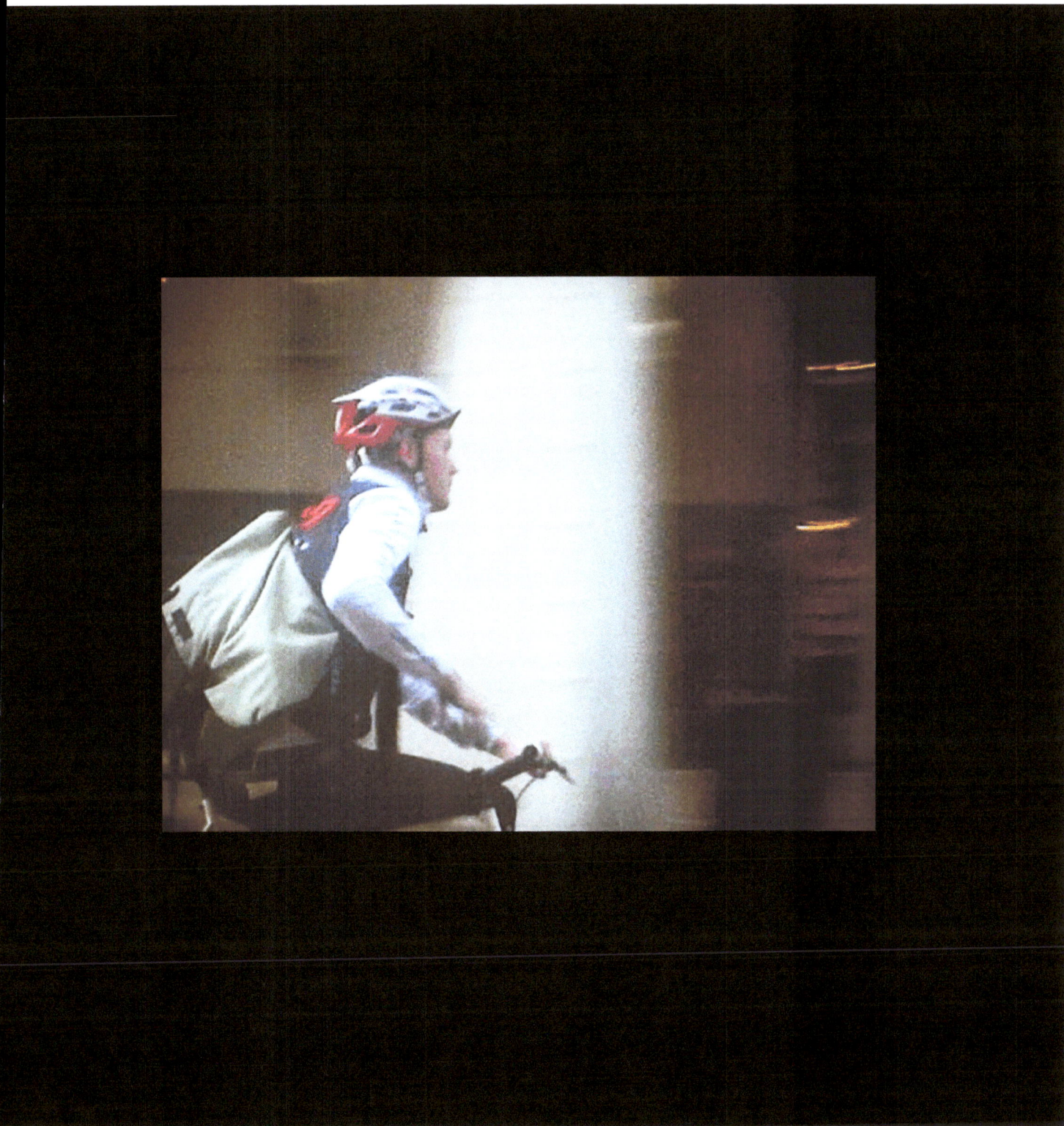

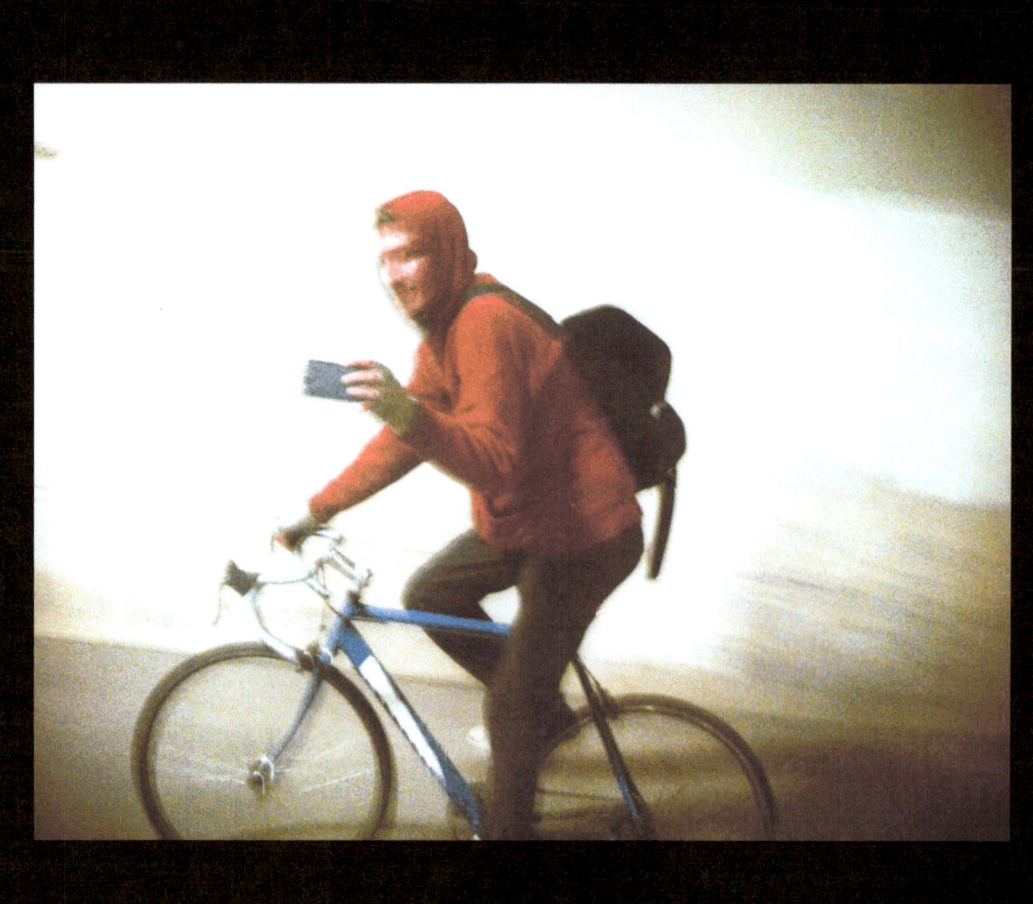

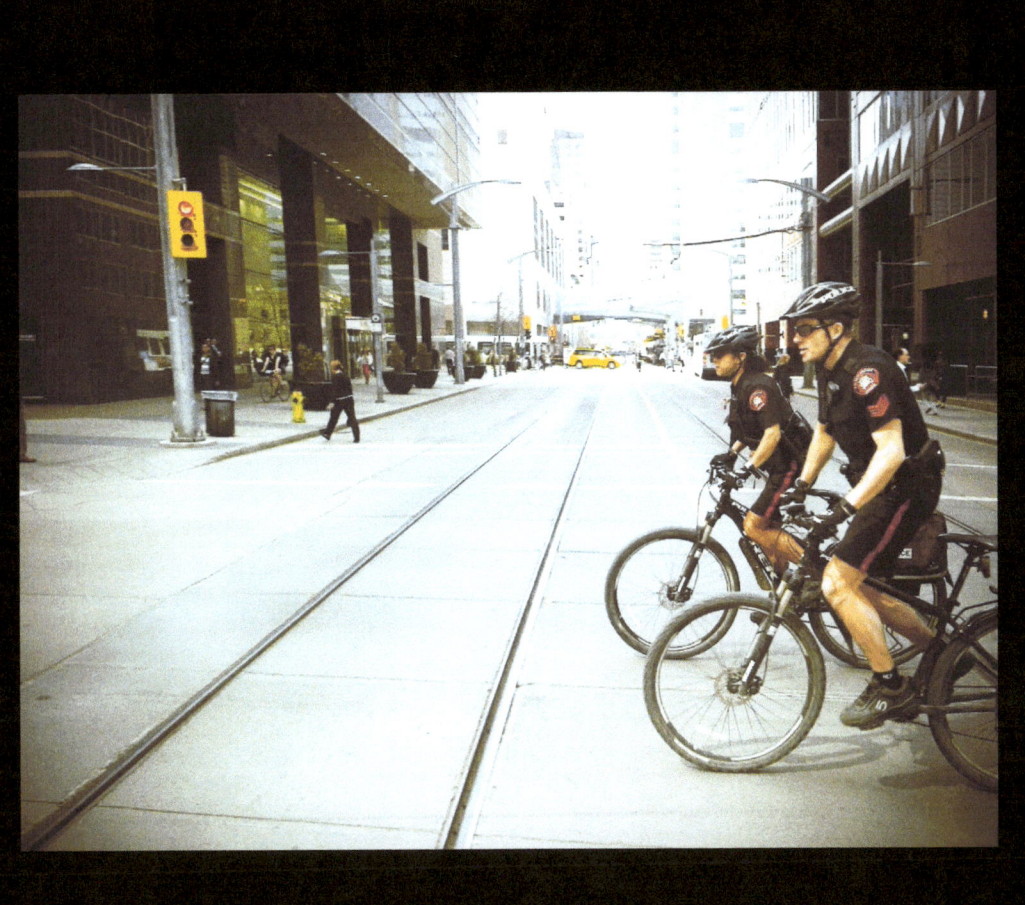

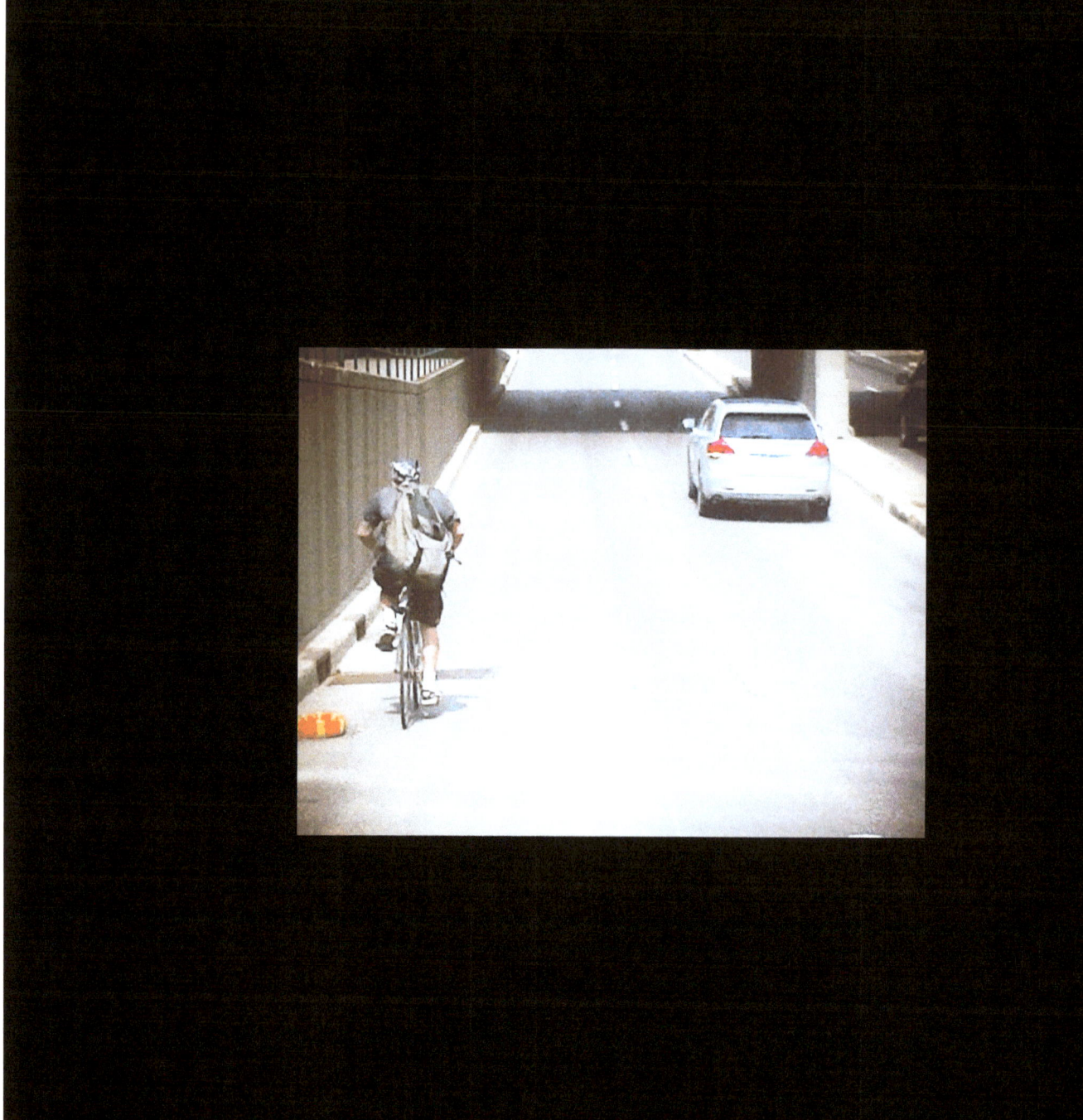

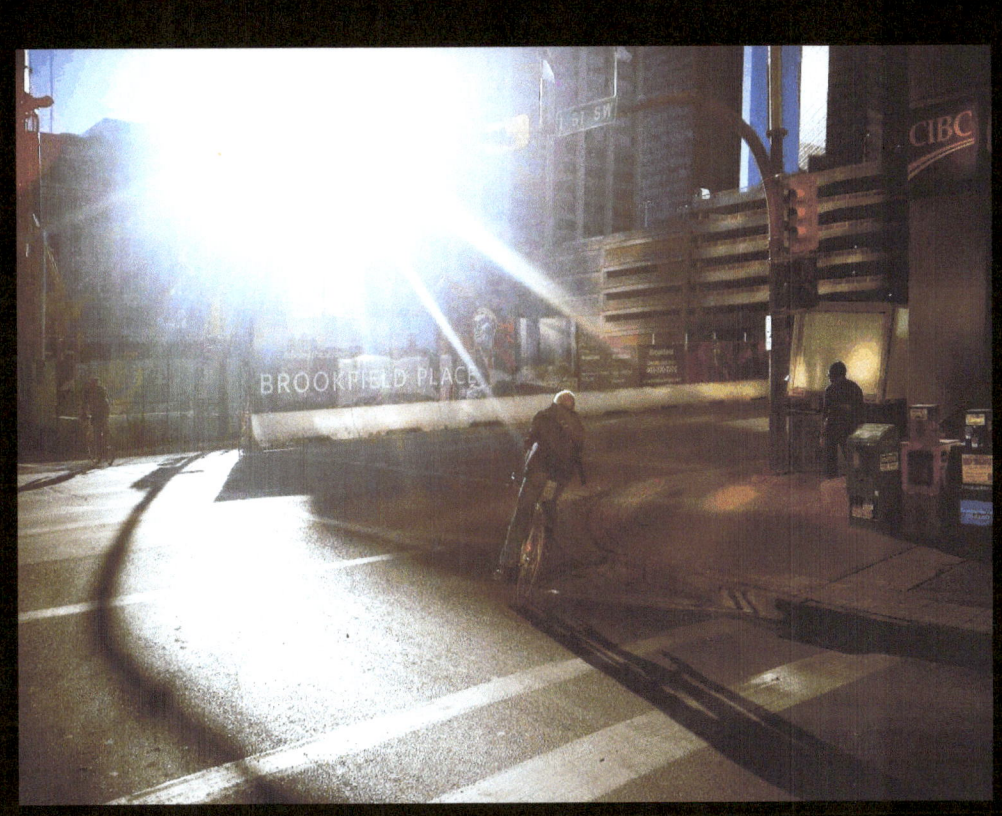

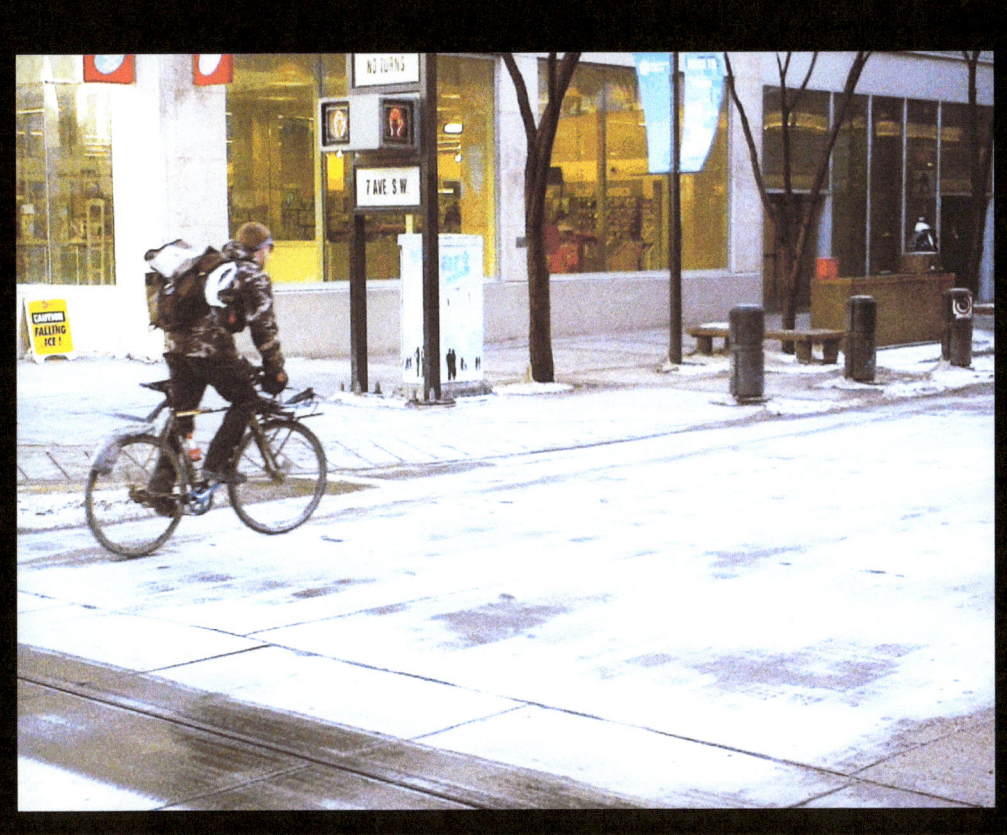

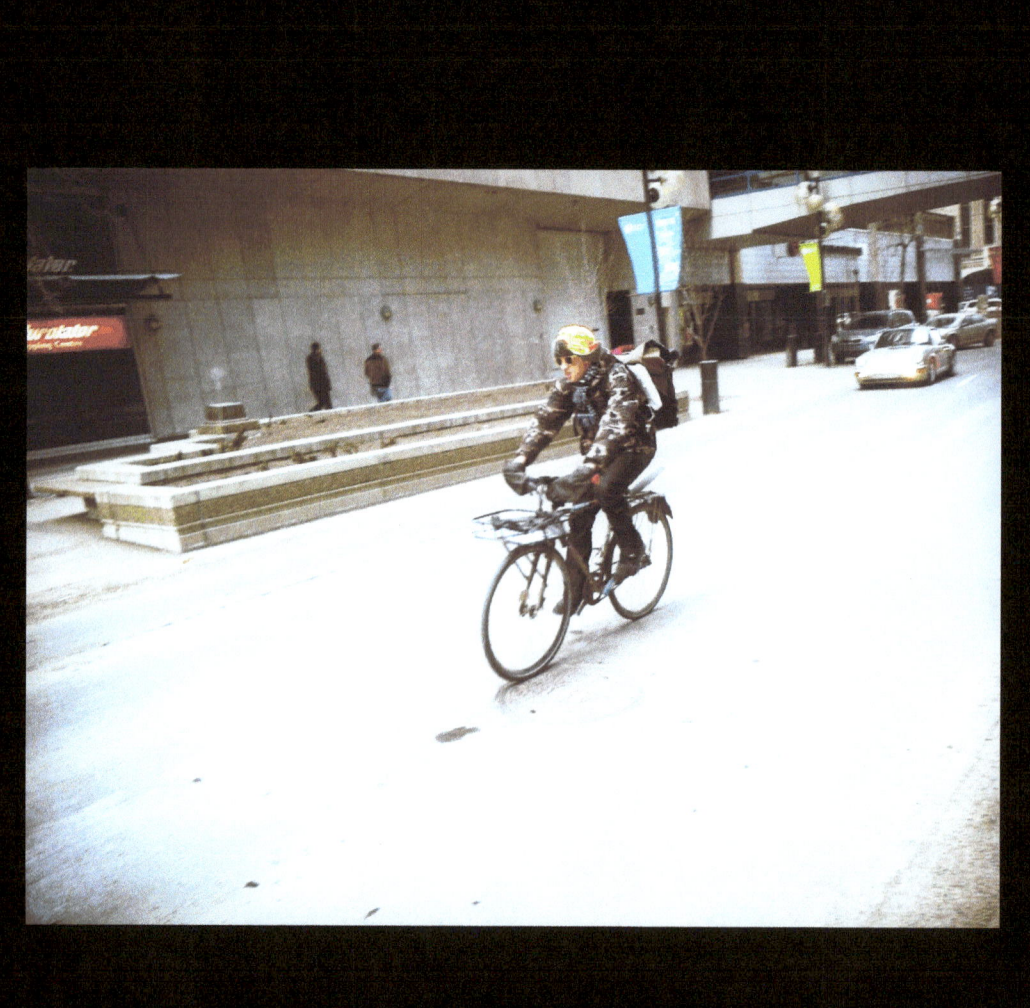

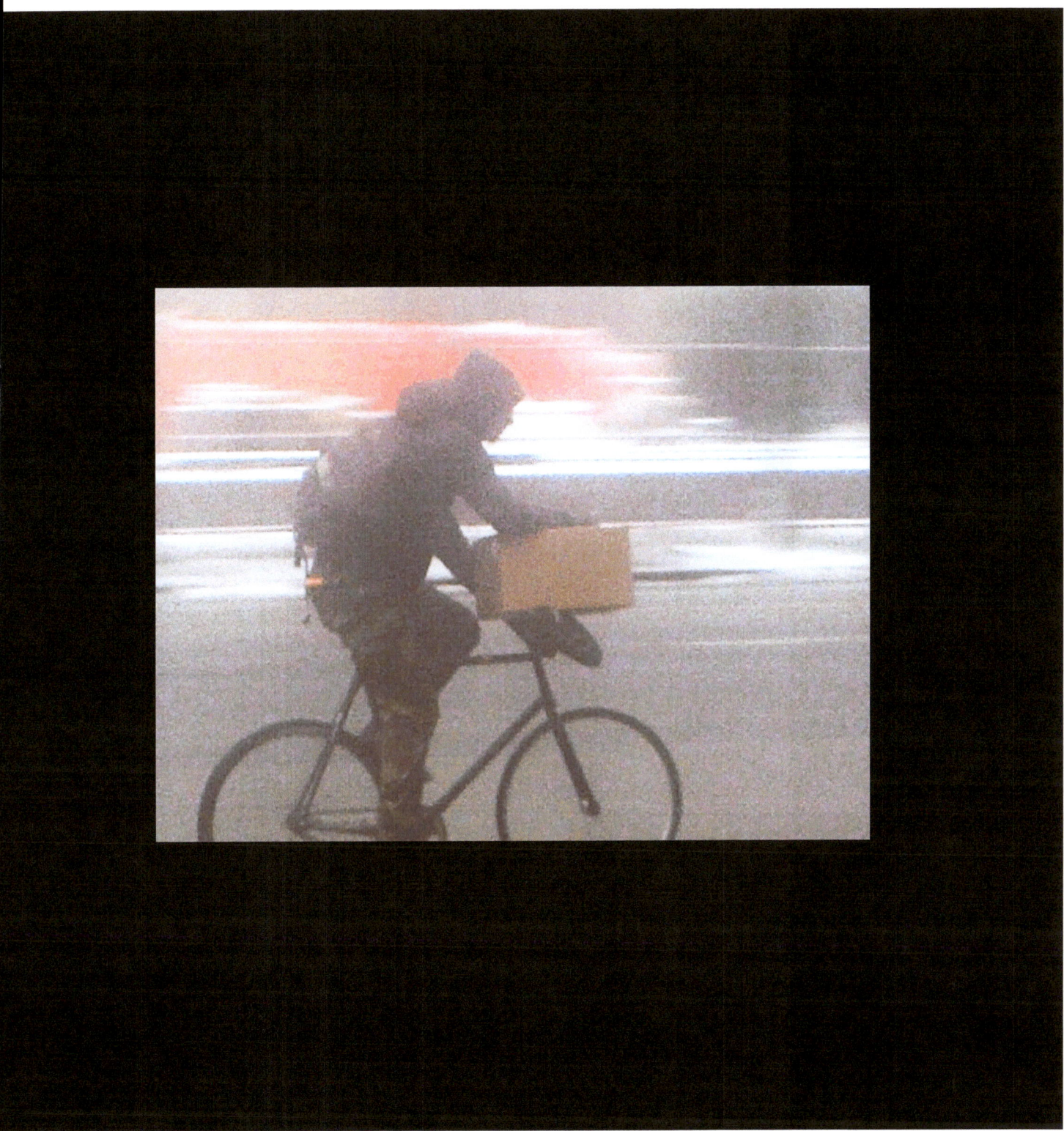

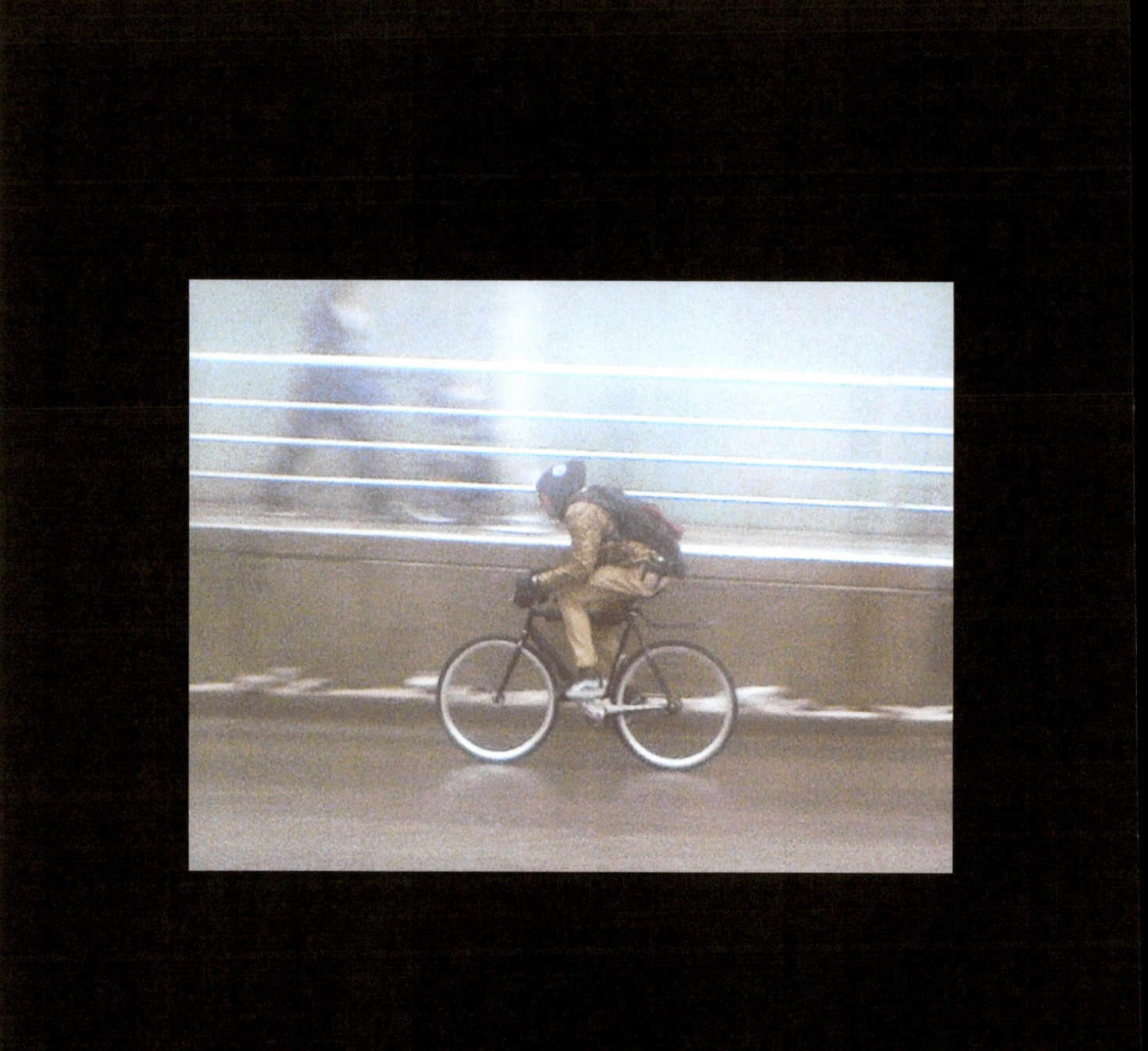

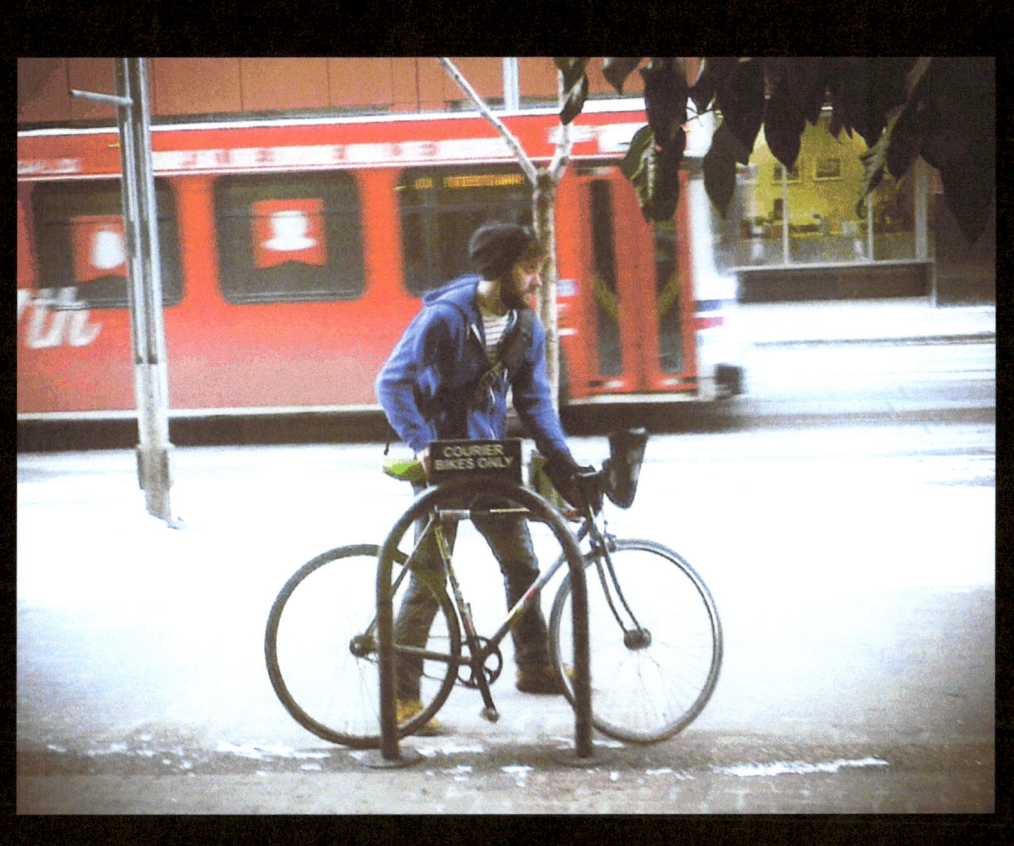

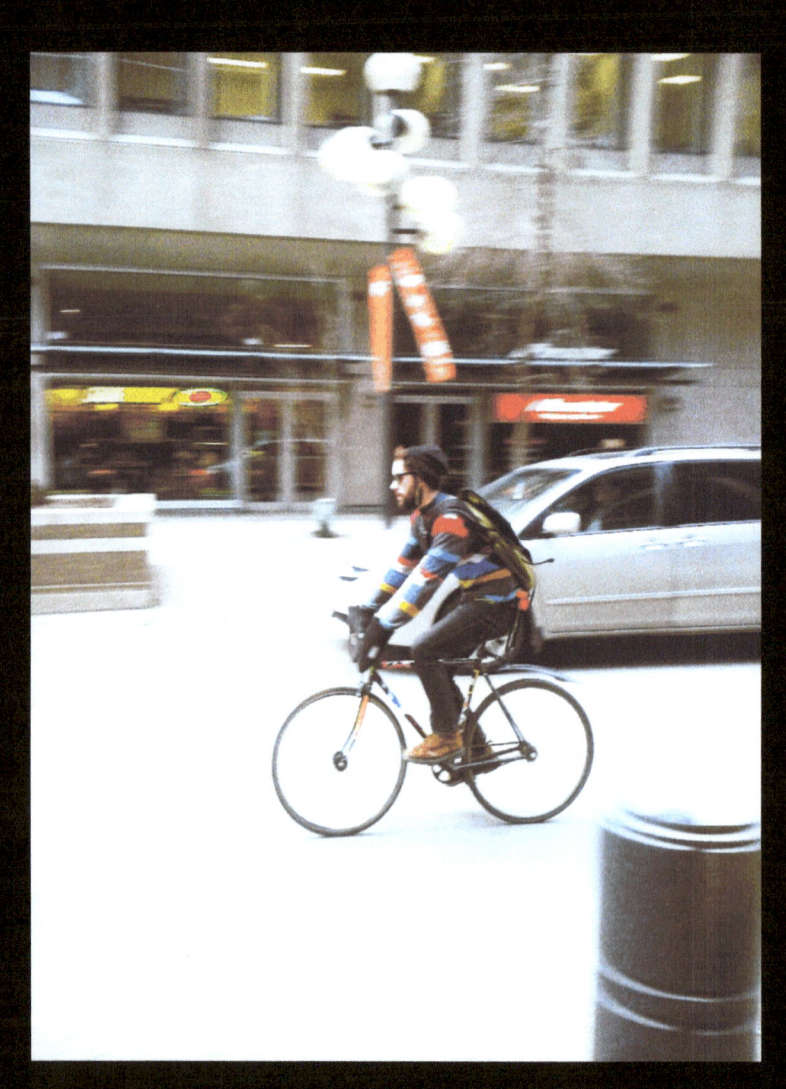

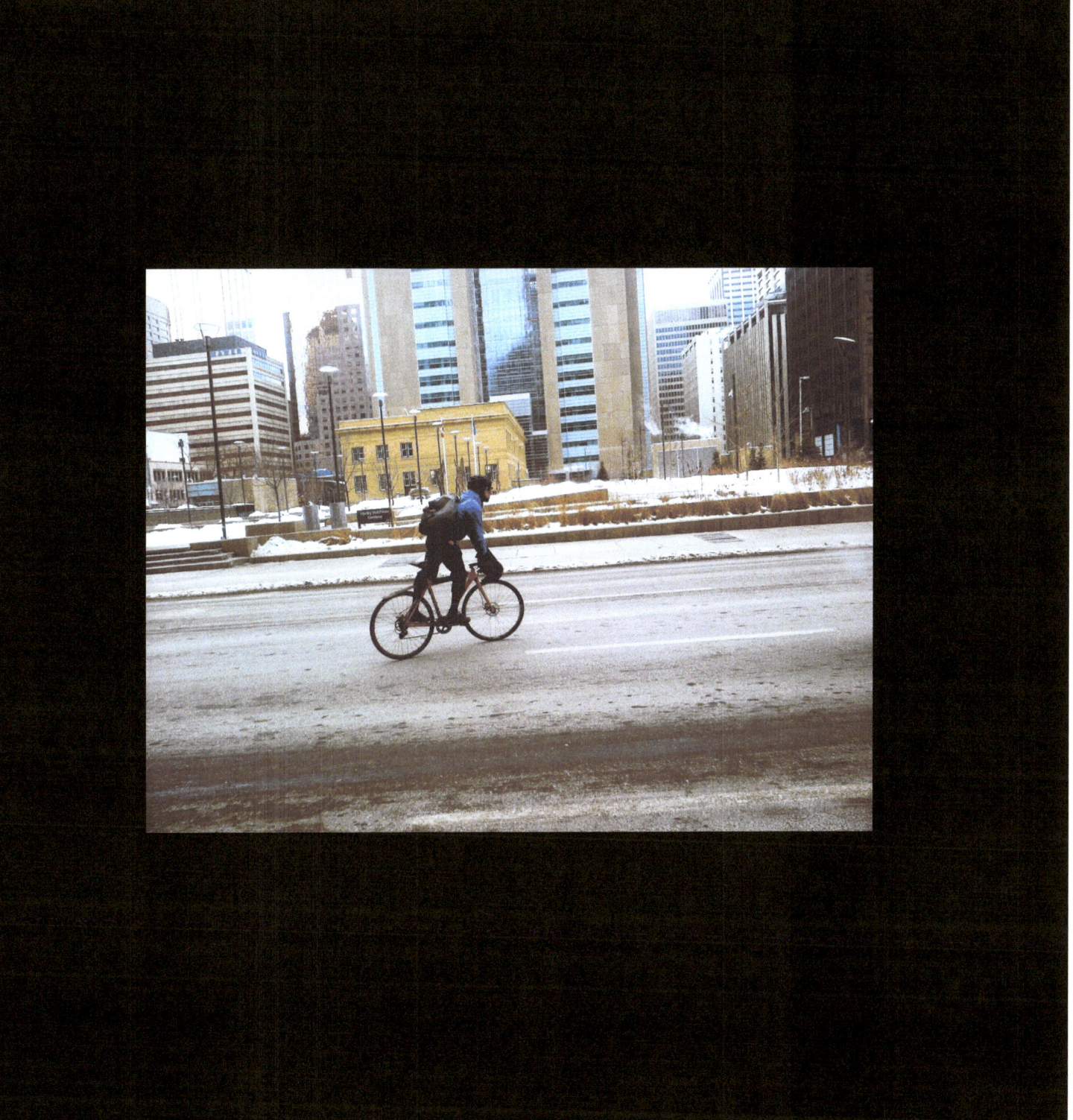

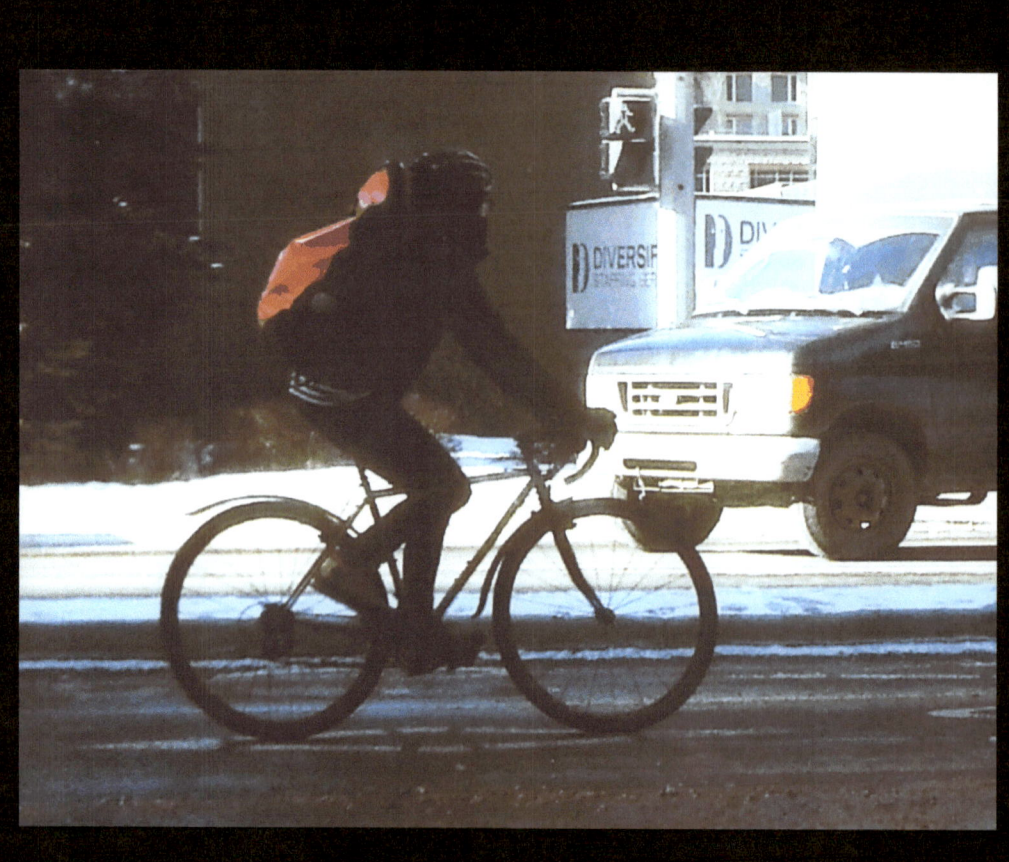

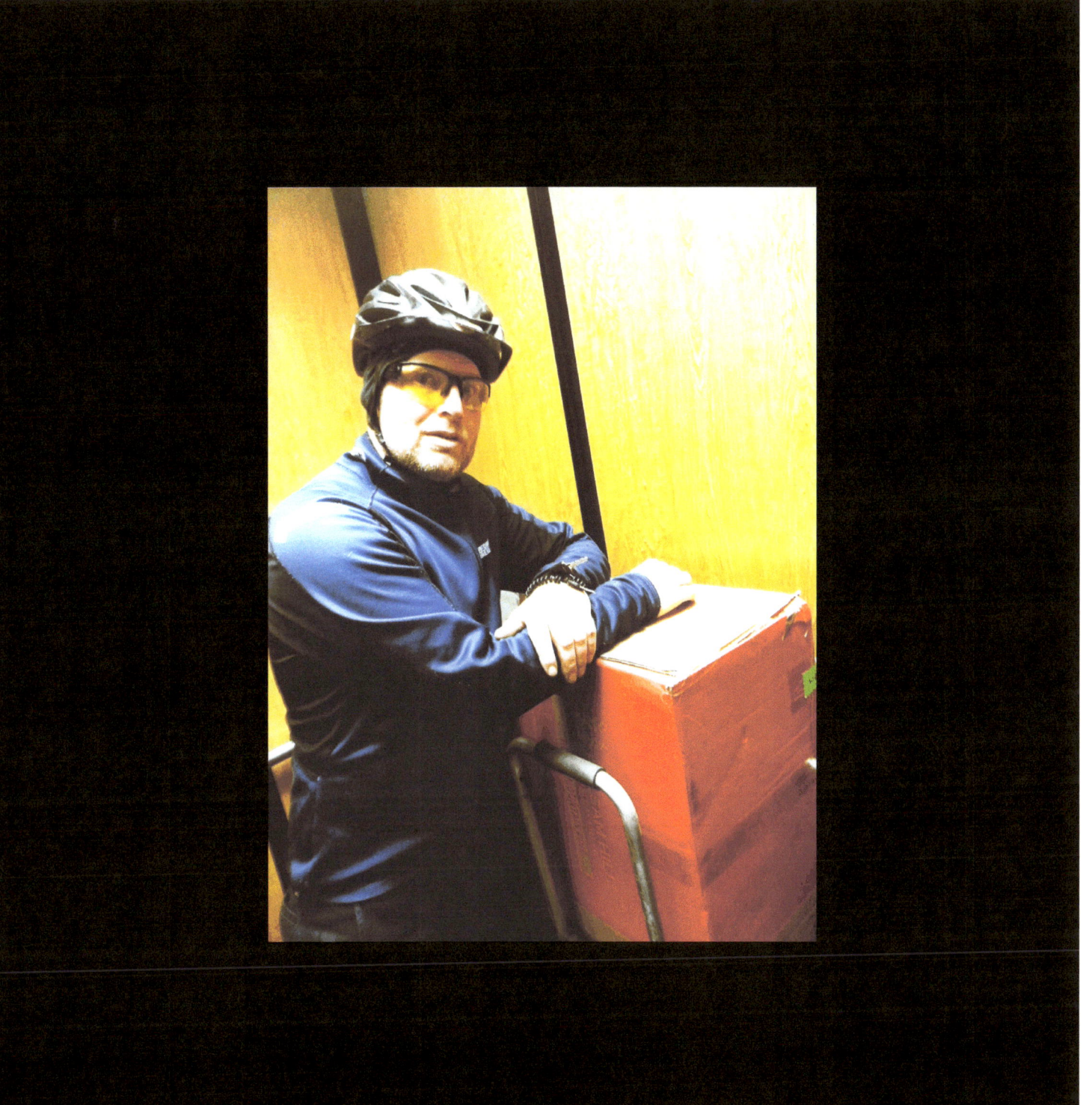

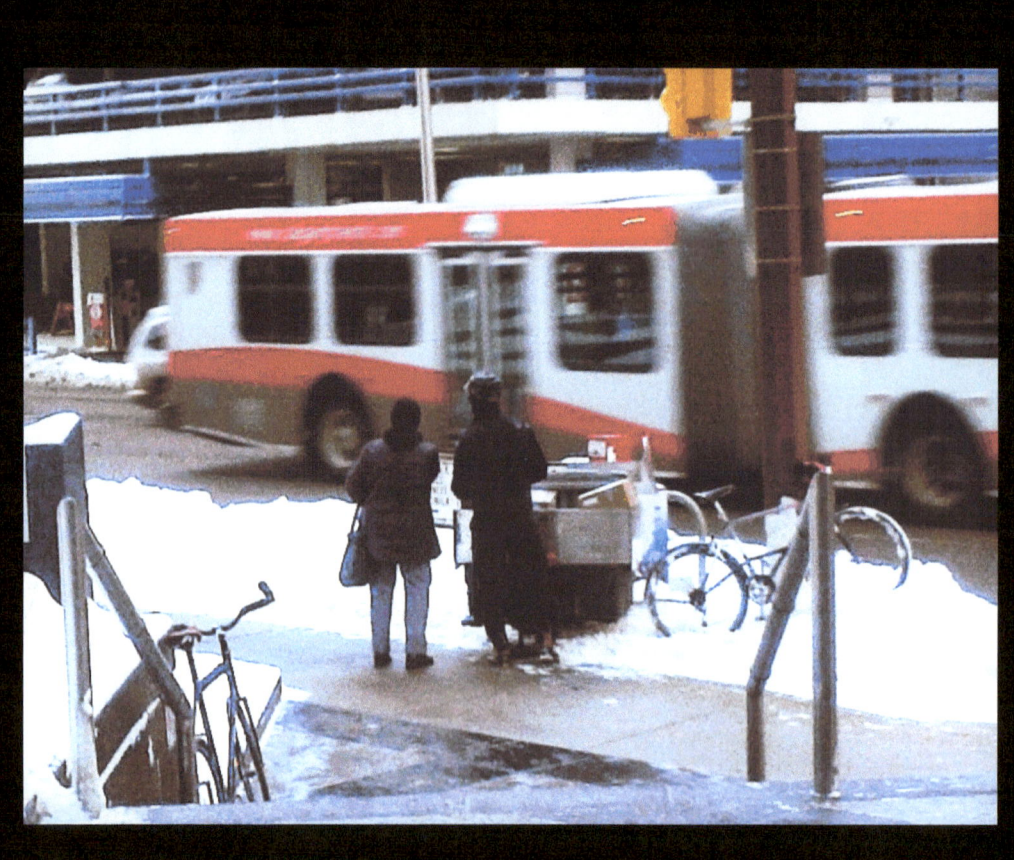

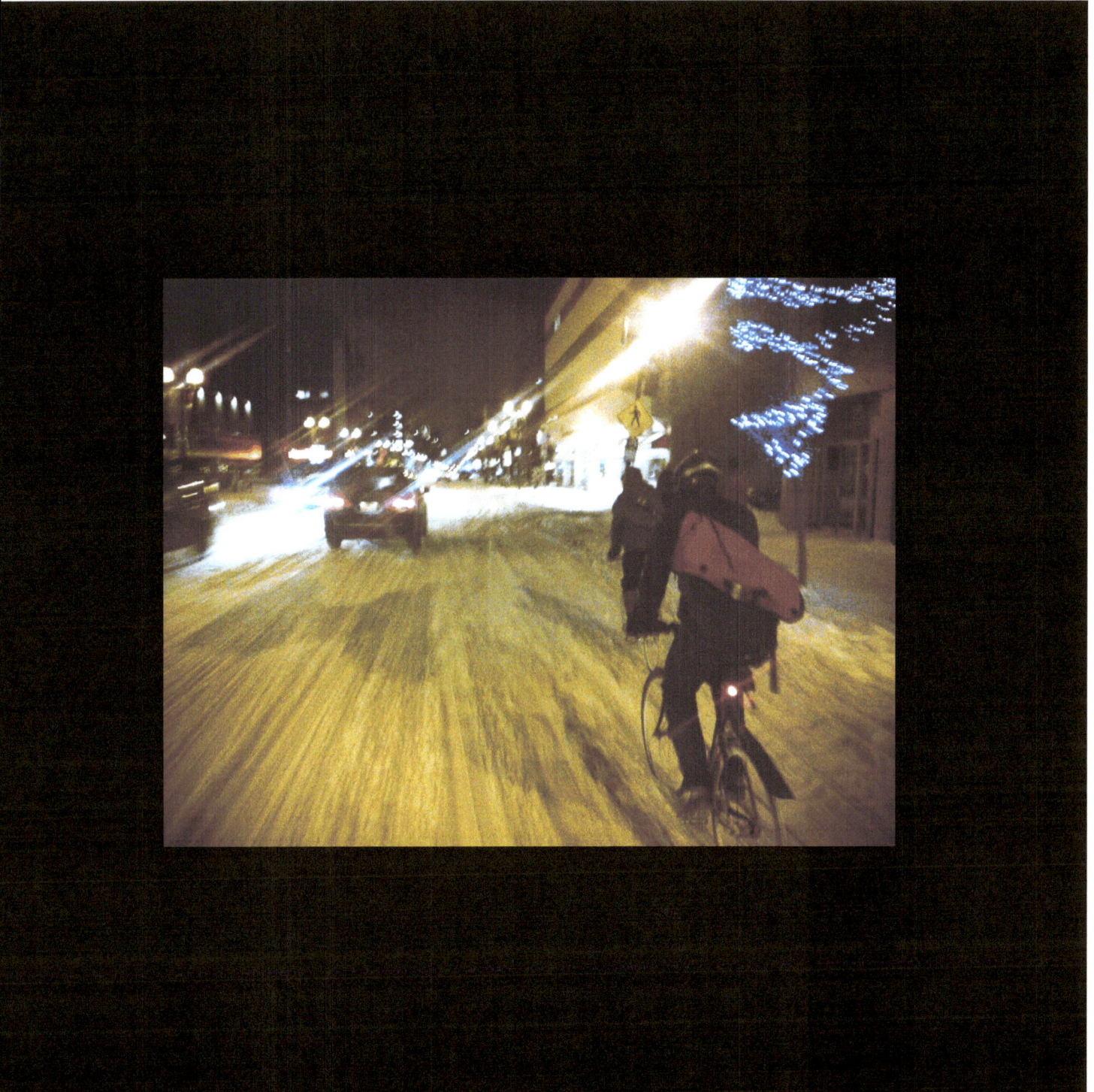

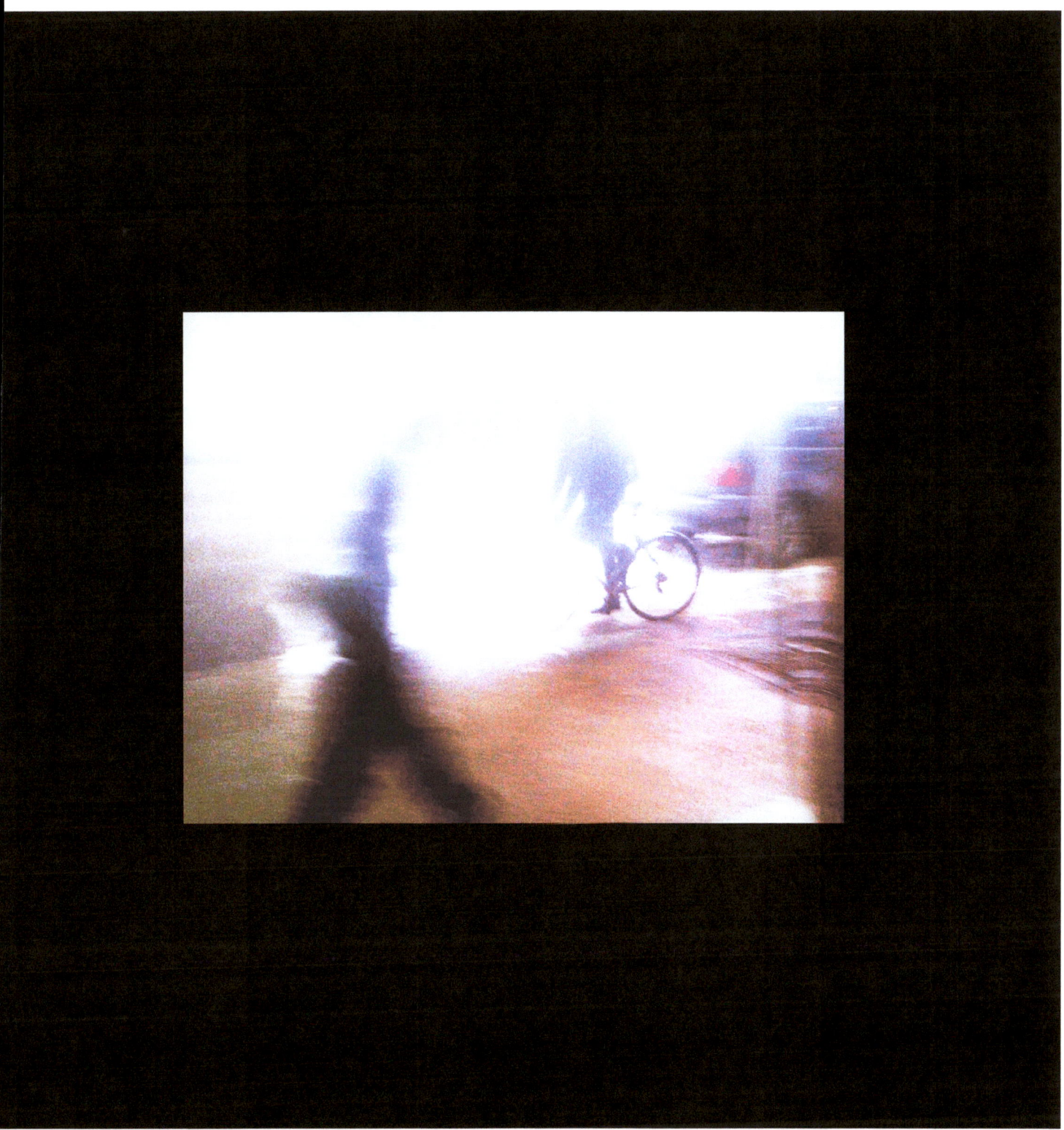

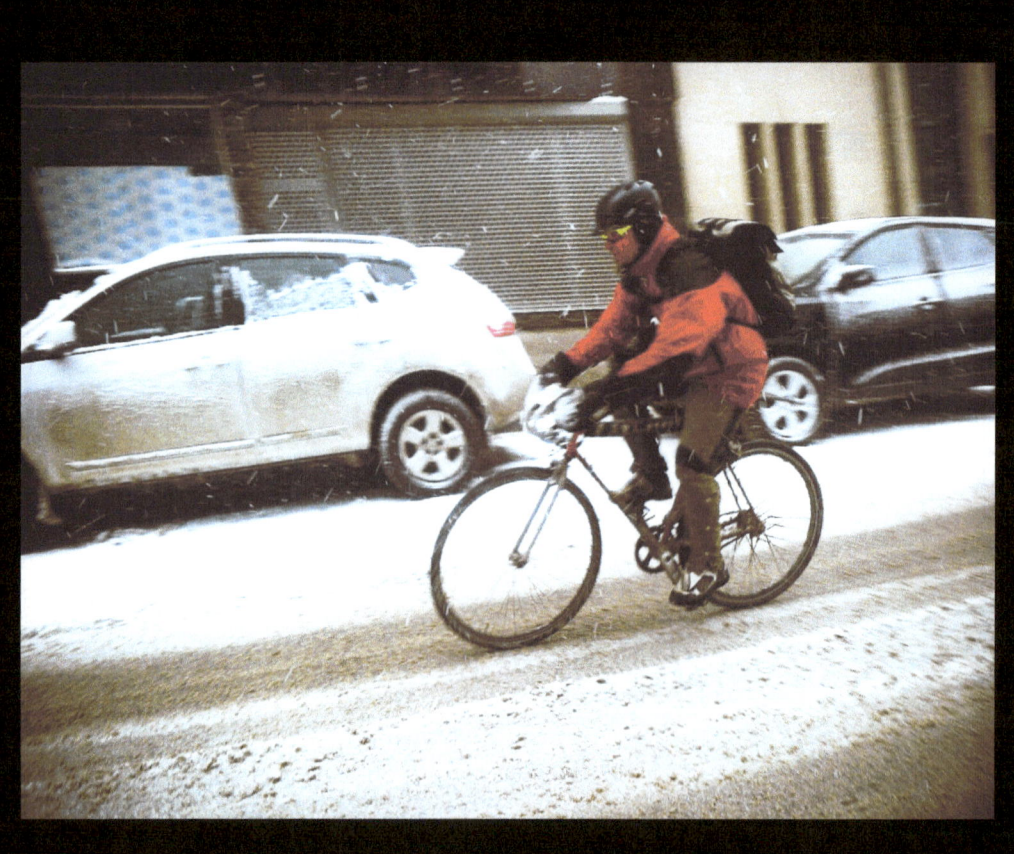

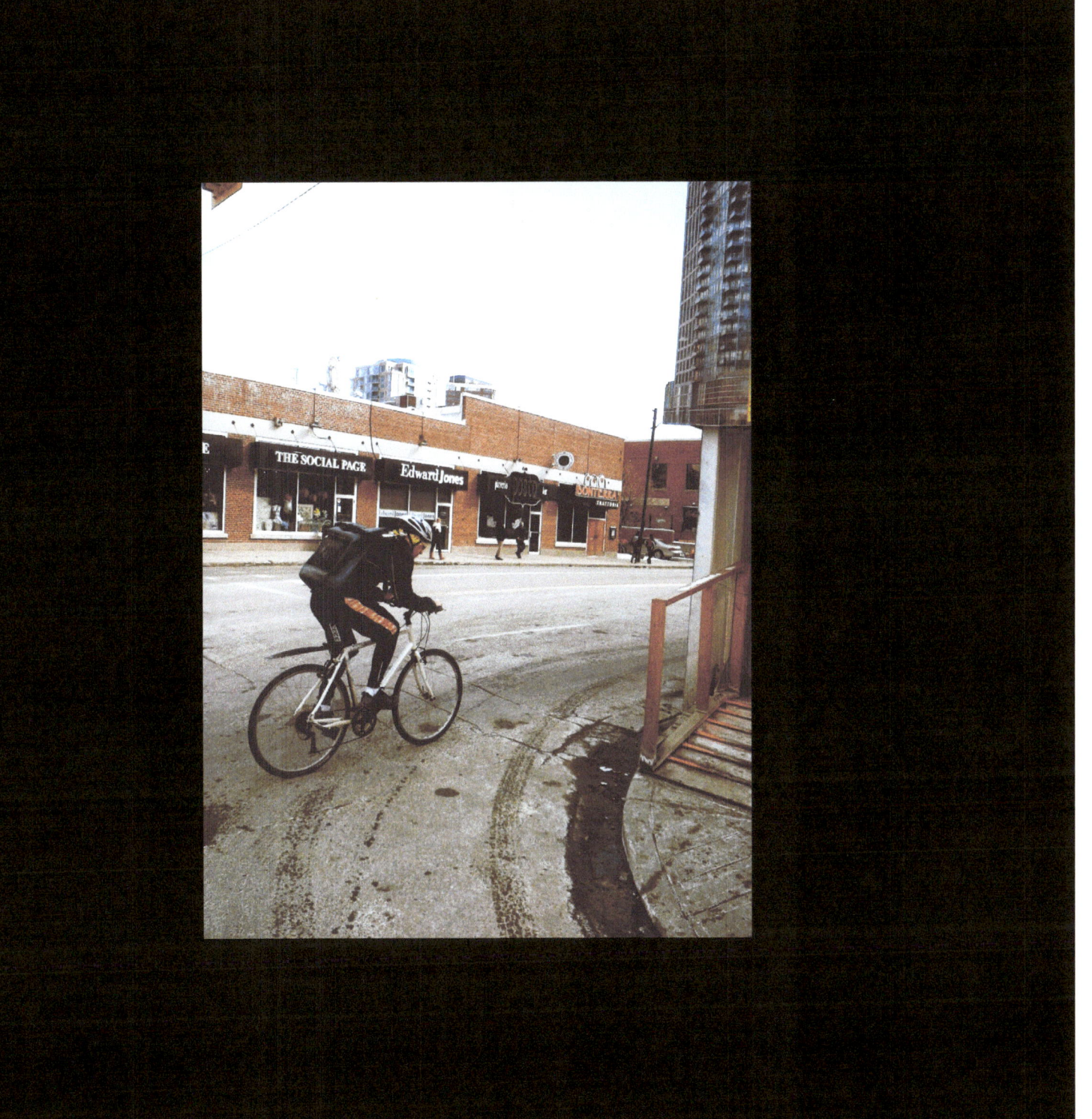

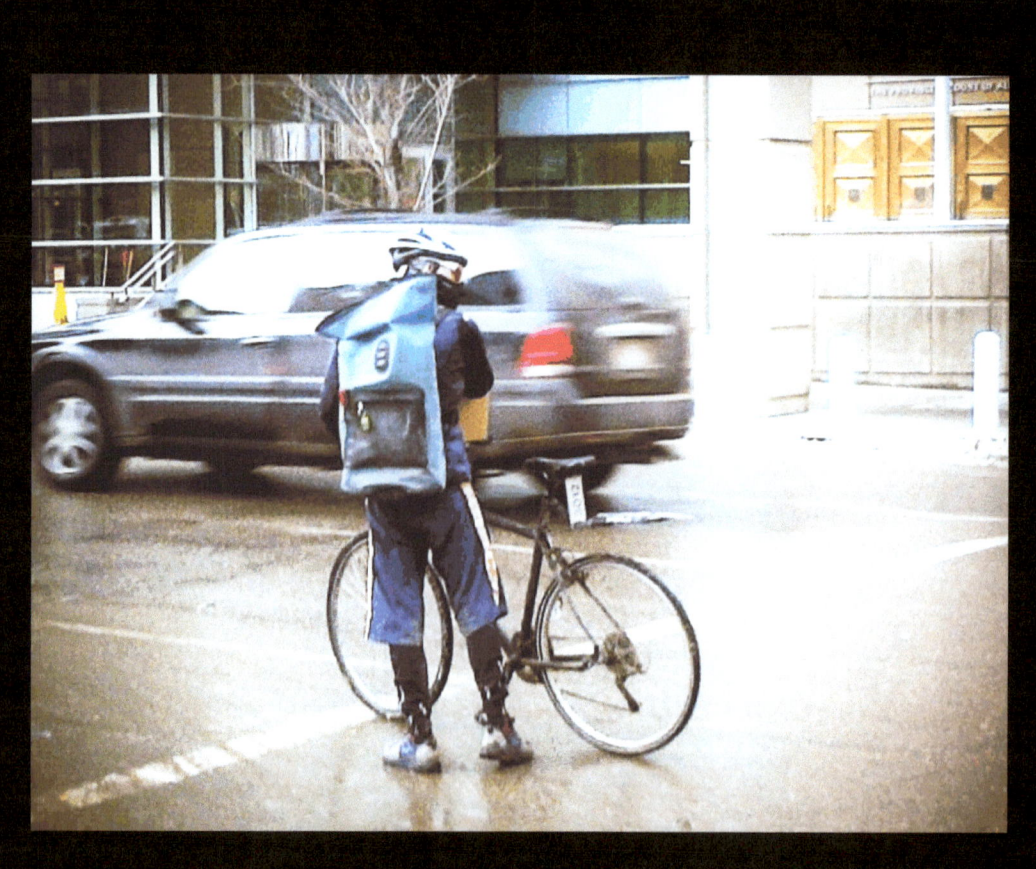

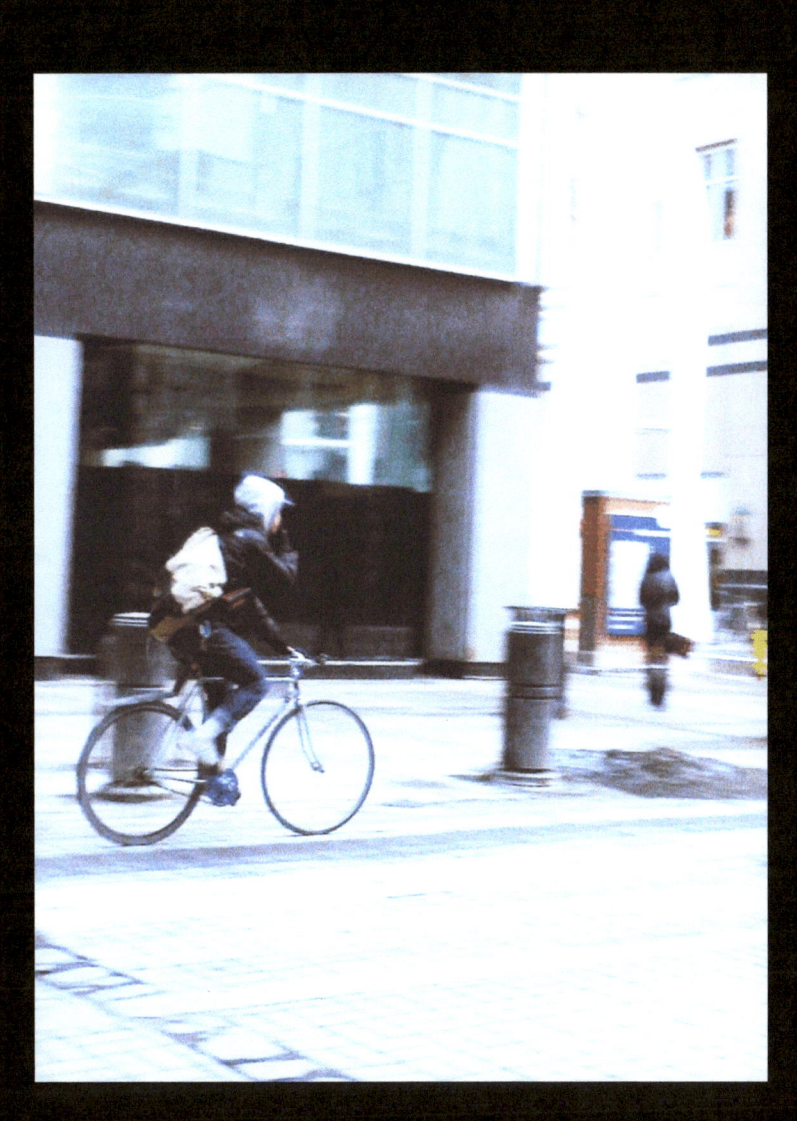

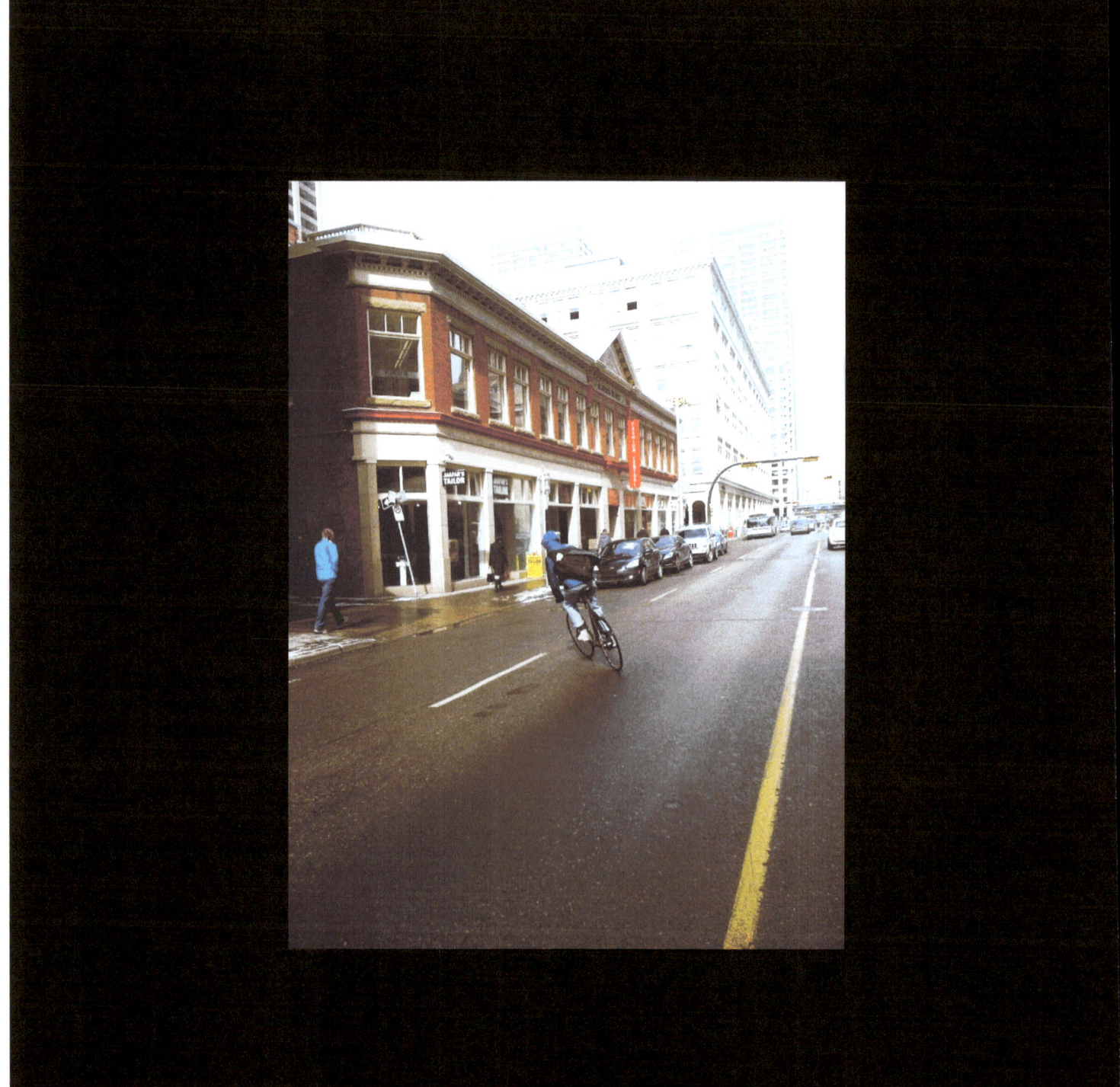

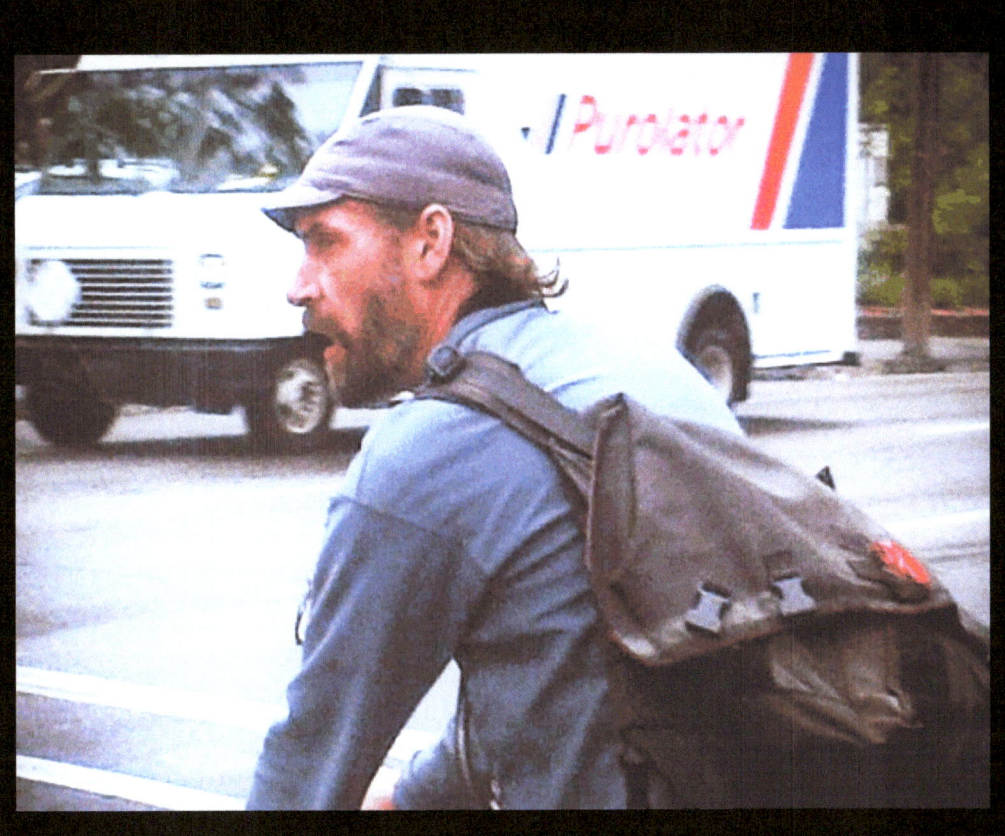

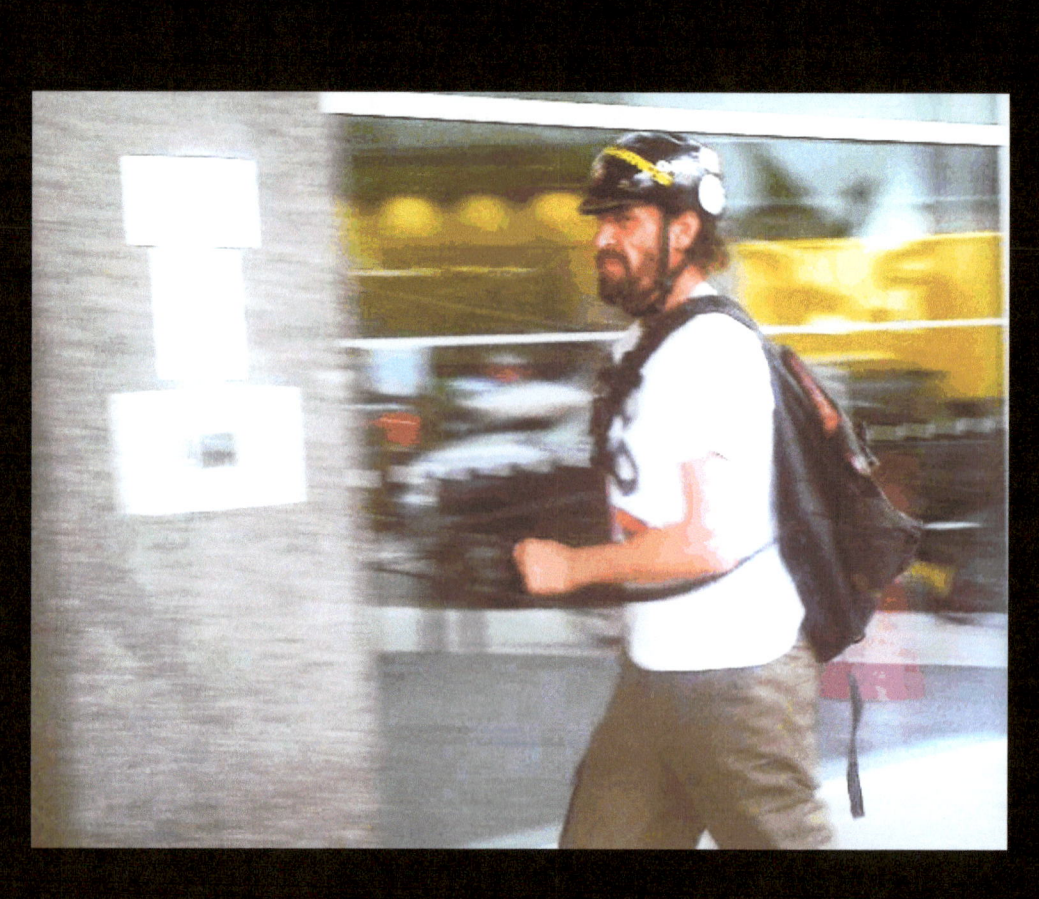

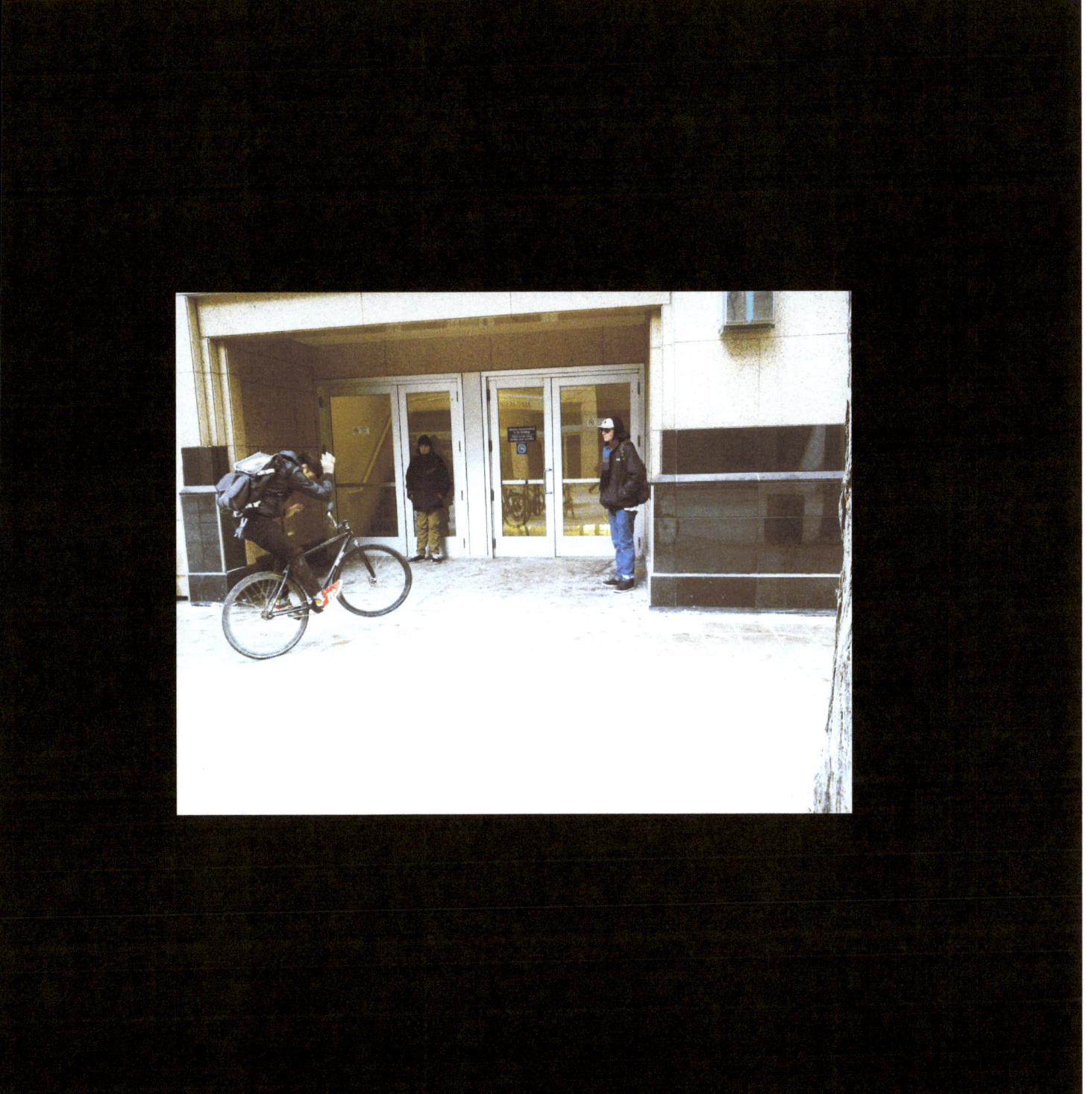

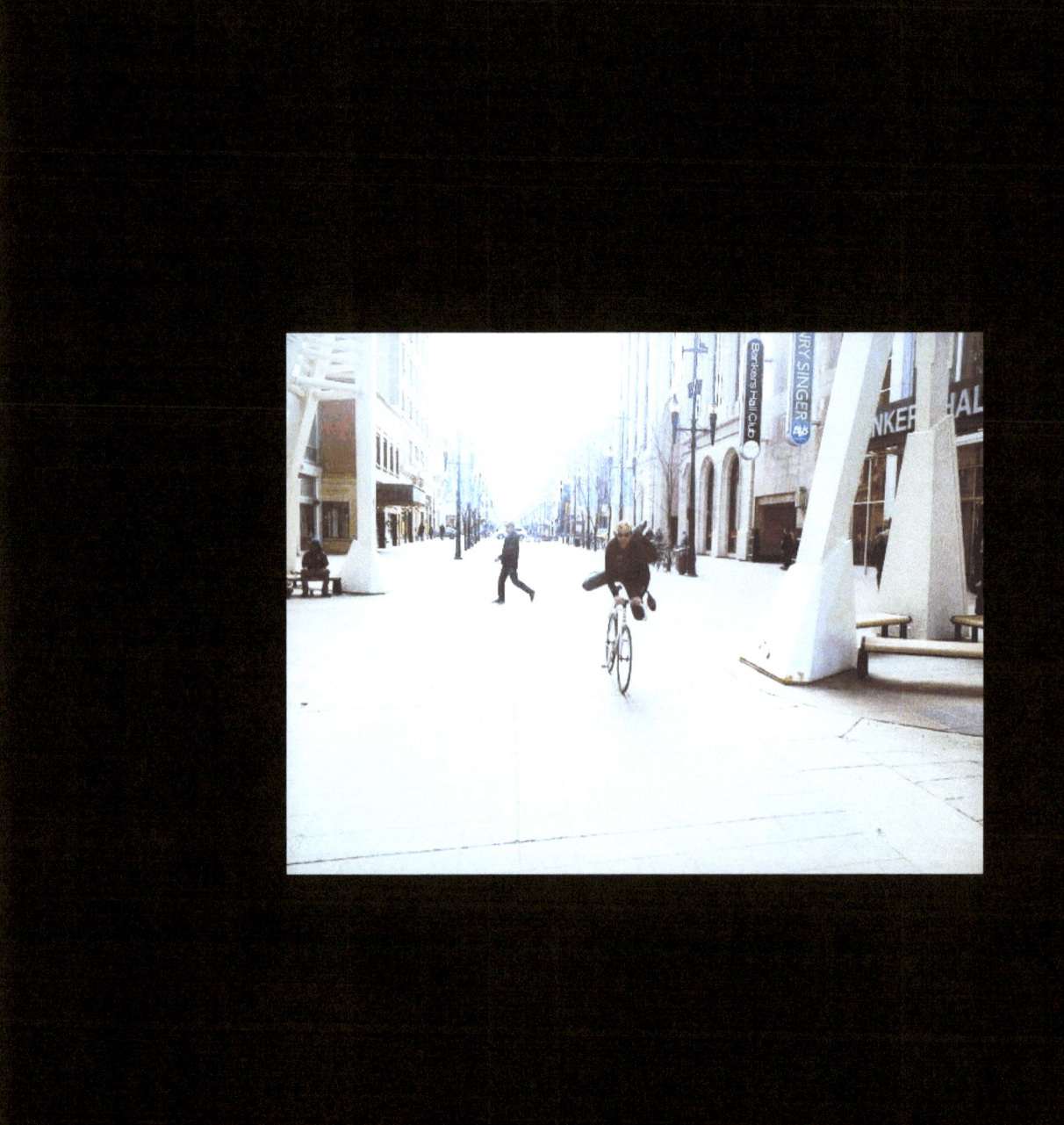

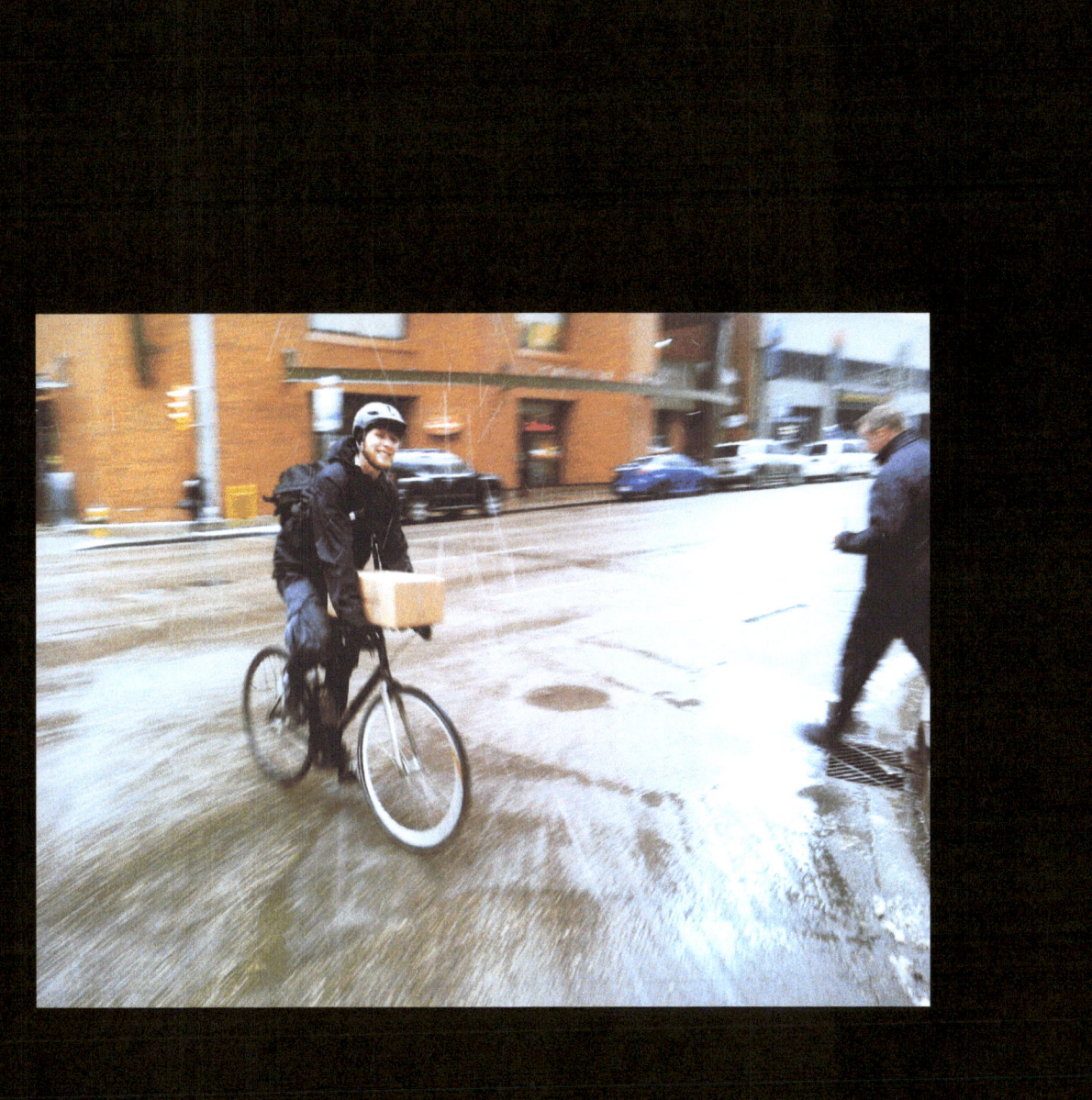

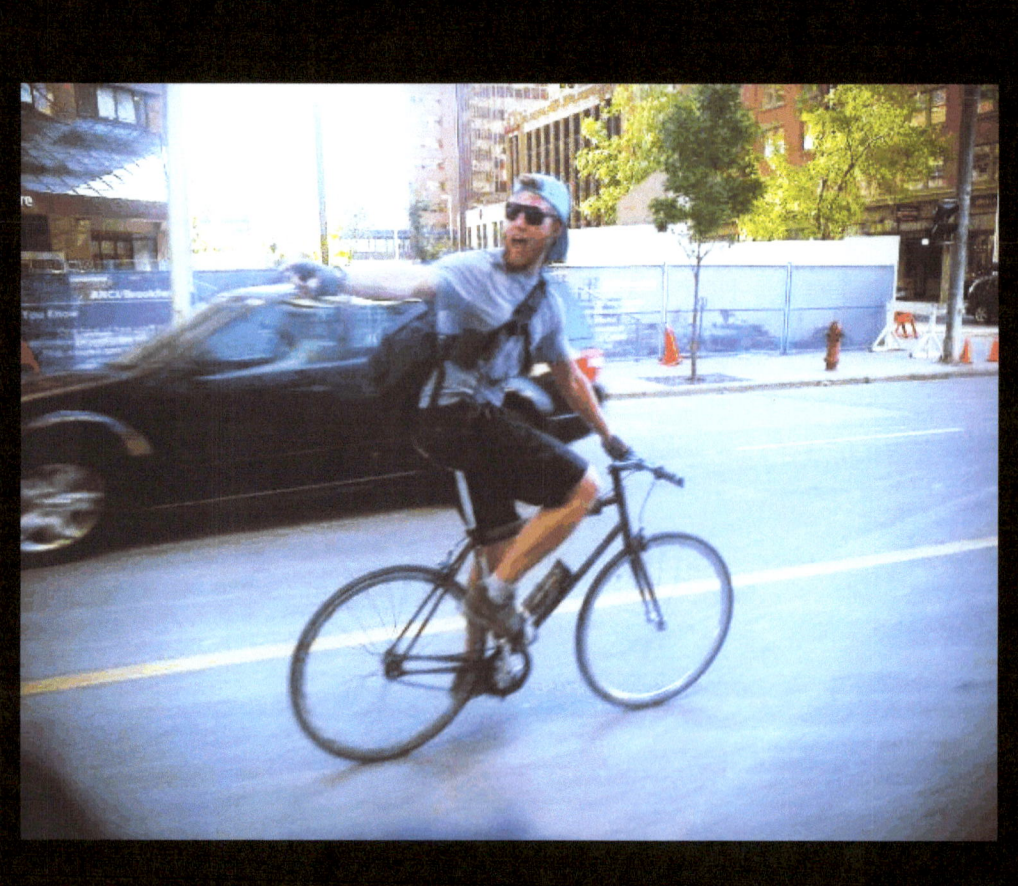

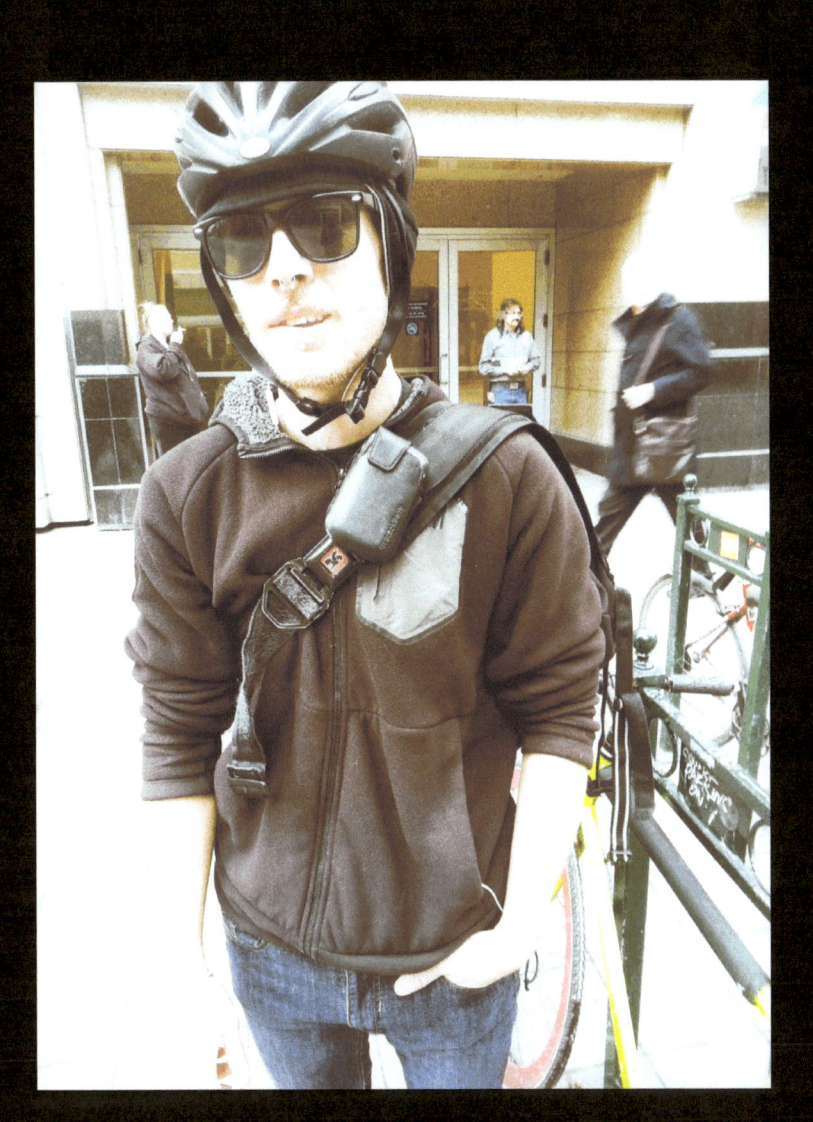

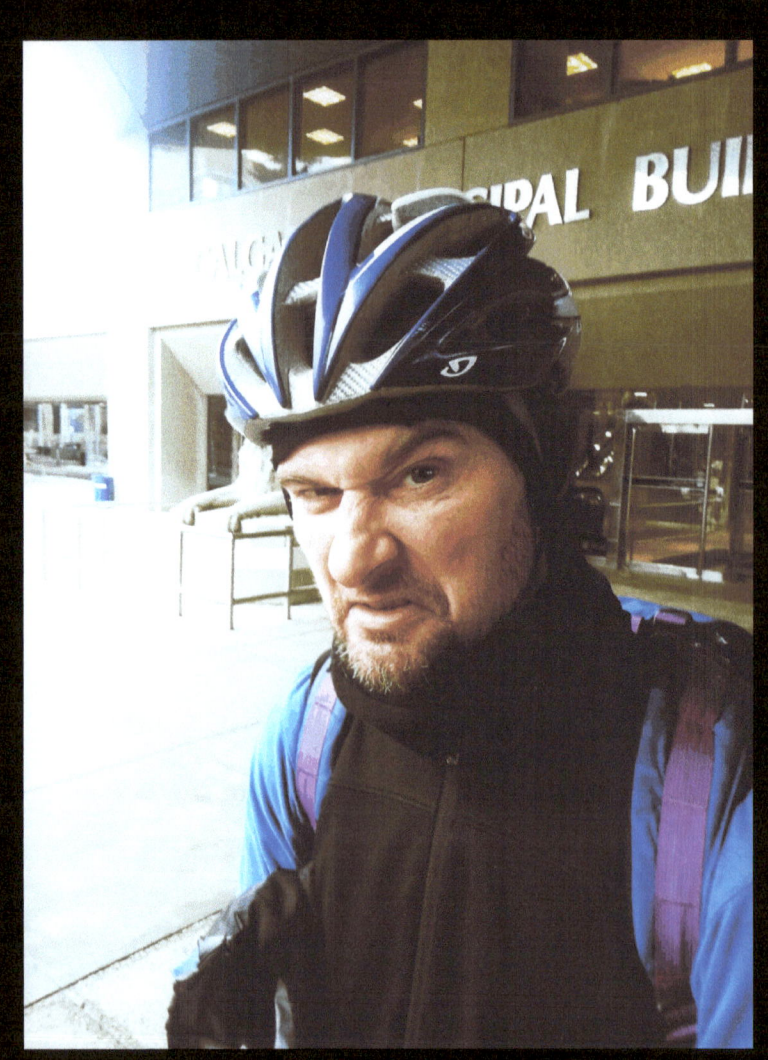

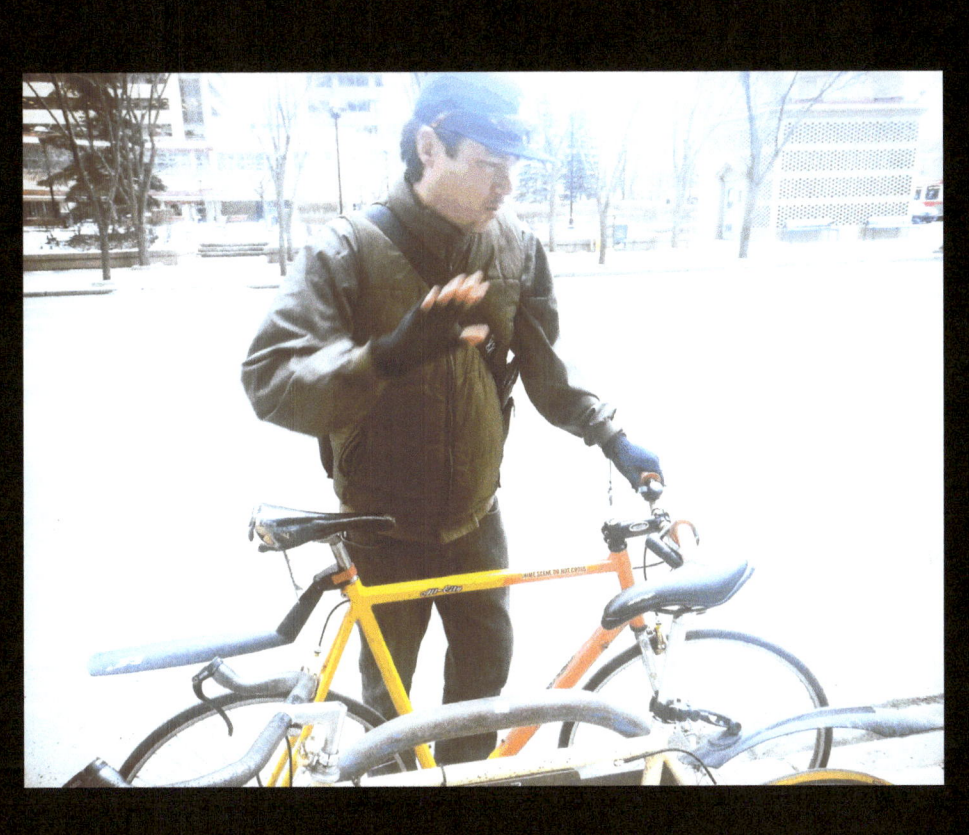

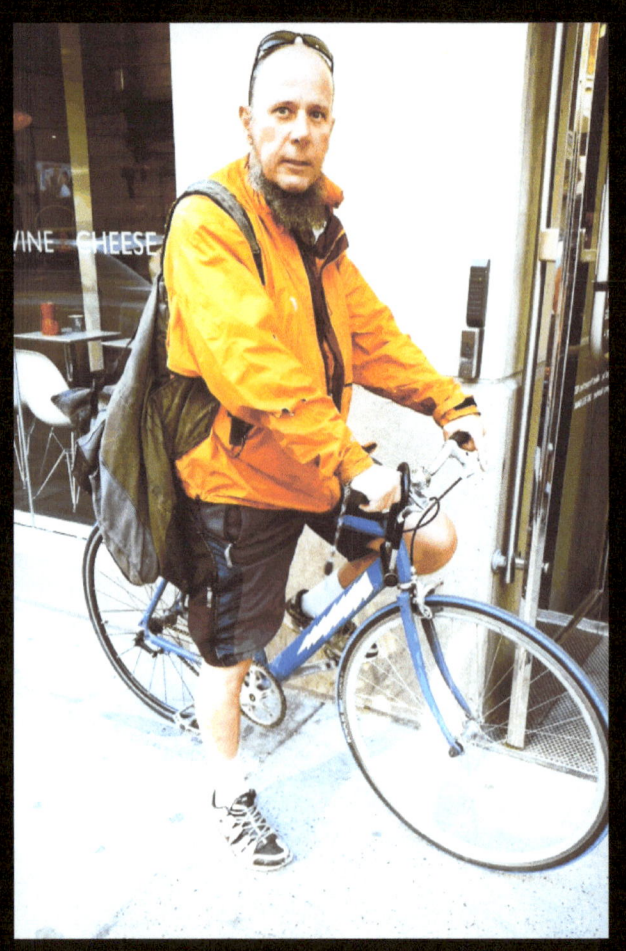

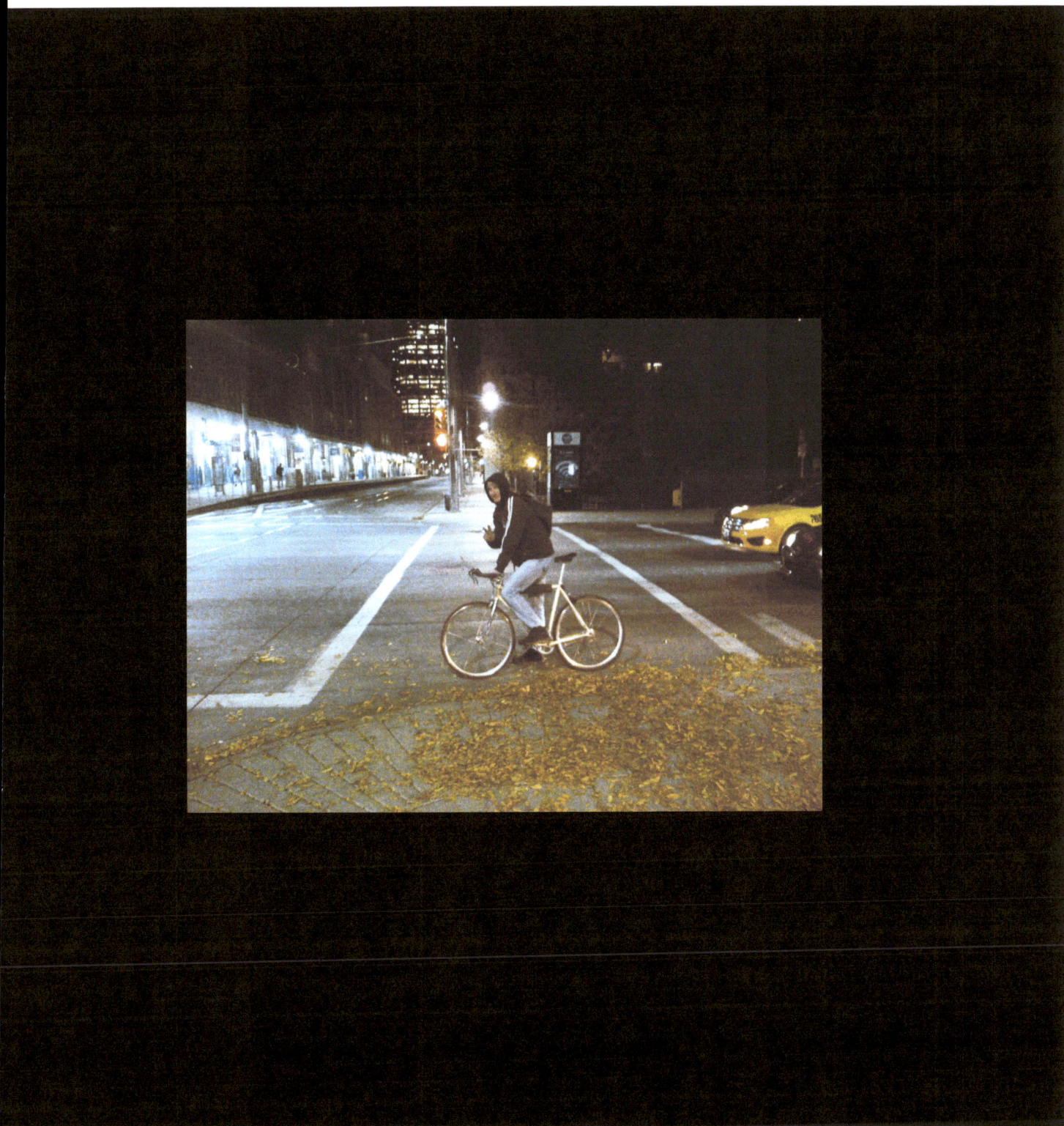

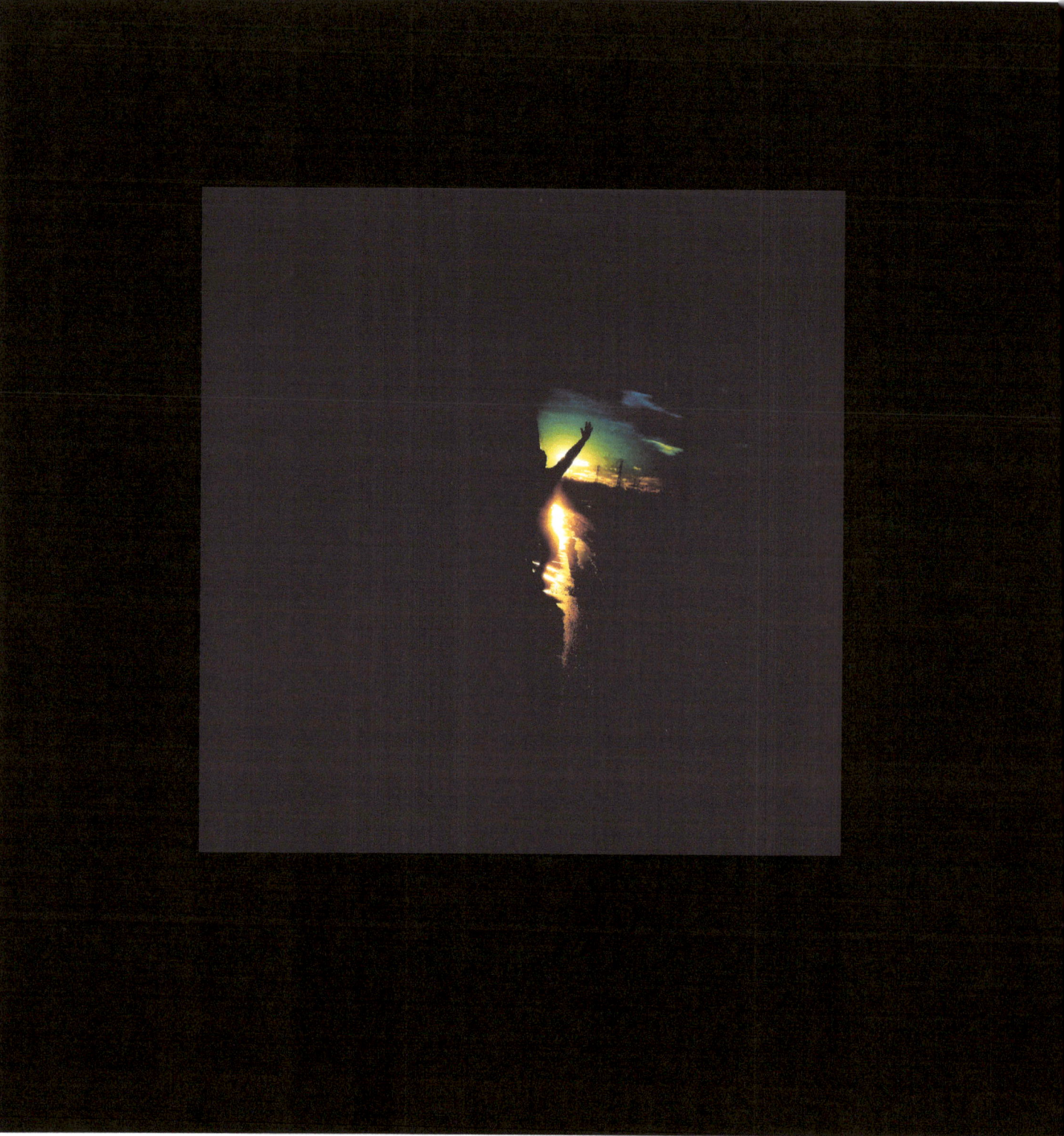

www.ingramcontent.com/pod-product-compliance
Lightning Source LLC
Chambersburg PA
CBHW051200220526
45473CB00003B/843